Dedication

The book is dedicated to my three children, Jennifer, Stephen and Andrew who are my heroes. They are always there for me, never hesitating to offer their love and support any time of the day or night. They are my true and genuine inspiration.

Cover Design and Illustrations / Amber Luecke

Published by Hallard Press LLC

Publisher's Cataloging-in-Publication data

Names: Welsh, Barbara C., author. | Luecke, Amber, illustrator.

Title: Picture perfect: poems about the memories of life / by Barbara C. Welsh; illustrated by Amber Luecke.

Description: The Villages, FL: Hallard Press LLC, 2024.

Identifiers: LCCN: 202491179

ISBN: 978-1-962326-38-4 (Paperback)

Subjects: LCSH Poetry, American. | BISAC POETRY / American / General | POETRY / Subjects &; Themes / Family | POETRY / Women Author

Classification: LCC PS3623.E4825 O54 2022 | DDC 811.6--dc23

PICTURE PERFECT
Poems About the Memories of Life

BARBARA WELSH

TABLE OF CONTENTS

Poems About the Memories of Life 1

PART 1

Sending You a Garden 3

CHAPTER 1

Little Drops of Hope 11

CHAPTER 2

Picture Perfect...17

Mack and Cheese...27

Don't Tell Me I Can't Dance Anymore 37

A Safety Net 45

Hanging Just By A Thread 55

A Bright Crescent Moon 63

CHAPTER 8

Jars of Clay 69

CHAPTER 9

Dancing on the Edges of Your Heart 117

Icing on the Cake 125

Just Because It's Raining 133

The Wonderful Wizard.. 157

PART 2

OTHER BOOKS BY BARBARA WELSH

One Bright Day
Poems about the Dances of Life
Illustrated by Donna Yankus

Sell Yourself a Smile
Poems About the Smiles of Life
Illustrated by Catharine Mannion

Poems About the Memories of Life

PART 1

Sending You a Garden

CHAPTER 1

Sending You a Garden

I'm sending a garden to you
Hoping you'll understand what to do.
Unlike a forest it has structure and order
With room for growth minus the disorder
Ensuring a more productive life for tomorrow
Along with hope for a world without sorrow.
From the abundance of resources that God provides
You will find all you need to survive and thrive.
If wise and resourceful, you will learn how to heal
As you discover all that is natural and real.
If you take tender care of your garden it will grow
While your spirit and mind gains new knowledge to bestow.
Cultivating a garden will initiate a revival or cleansing
A renewal or rebirth that is gradually ascending.
Your garden creates an interdependence with nature
A blending of your work with that of the creator
Symbolizing the abundance of all God offers to us
When you take the effort to learn and trust.
I hope you will care for this garden a little each day
And discover all the ways God's love is displayed.

The Source of Enthusiasm

Where does enthusiasm come from
Does it come from a beat of a drum
When you are having a lot of fun
Or when you feel love in your heart
Hoping it will never change or fall apart?
When God is the origin of good in our lives
It creates a type of joy that is very precise——
An experience of genuine contentment
Perceived as pleasantly resplendent.
The heart of God becomes visible
When we show love that is inexplicable,
Through our actions and attentive regard
For one another; not blemished or marred.
God's love is reflected in our ability to care
With compassion and a willingness to share.
A source of enthusiasm can be frivolity and merriment
And sometimes from rest and replenishment
Or an answer to prayer culminates in exuberance
Along with all blessings diverse and numerous.

Insights of the Wise

Learning to do what is right, just and fair
From the knowledge and wisdom of teachers who care.
Written a long time ago, Proverbs provide a gateway to truth
A book of instruction and inspiration for your own personal use.
No need to buy self-help books and instructional DVDs
When there is all that you need in each chapter and verse.
The theme of Proverbs is stated in chapter 1, verse 7, it is not in disguise
Only when a person trusts in God will they be truly wise.
Wise choices will watch over you, understanding keeps you safe.
As stated in Proverbs Chapter 2, verse 11, solid advice given in every case.
You'll find 31 chapters full of good examples and instructions all in one place
Study, reflect, take your time as you read at your own comfortable pace.
In chapter 18, verse 19 we are warned what should not ensue:
Spouting off before listening to the facts is both shameful and foolish to do.
In chapter 20, verse 29 we are told:
The glory of the young is their strength;
The gray hair of experience is the splendor of the old.
This is just the tip of the iceberg when it comes to what's in store.
The book of Proverbs is an instruction manual for life plus so much more.
Open a Bible, you'll be surprised and enlightened if you read a little each day.
It will alter the way you look at your life in most every way.
It's a Bible revival I heard Pastor Norman say
He calls it the happy book when you can look at it in that way.

Today, Tomorrow and Always

Learn from yesterday
In order to live life to the fullest today.
Then pray for the finest tomorrow
Aiming for happiness without sorrow.

You have the power to control your mood
With an abundance of people or in solitude.
Each day you arise and feel the morning sun
Until it sets and the day is done.

You have a chance to spread love and happiness
With a little courage, generosity and craftiness.
If you fell down yesterday then stand up today
It brings another opportunity to change your ways.

Today is yours to win or lose
It's up to you to decide what you choose.
If you get tied up with yesterday and tomorrow
Instead of focusing on today's agenda to follow
You may find yourself harried with too much to do
Getting stuck on a treadmill without an avenue.

Every day as the sun sets and rises
Start each day without pretense or disguises.
Let God lead you today, tomorrow and always
Throughout your life and into heaven's doorway.

Cultivating Your Garden

While walking in safe green pastures
Your eyes will begin to capture
The serenity and peace
That nature will release.

Smell the fresh grass growing
As soft rain begins flowing
Providing an environment for growth
So that the land can fulfill its oath.

Remnants of a dry desert will be gone
When your heart sings its own song
And the lyrics encourage Mother Earth
To call on God to bring forth new birth.

What does your garden grow
Will it have a harvest to show?
To help nourish the body as a whole
Along with the mind, spirit and soul.

If you trust God with faithfulness
Your garden will be blessed
Cultivating hope, love and goodness
While laying down roots of forgiveness.

Little Drops of Hope

CHAPTER 2

Little Drops of Hope

Nothing seems to be quite the same
It's a different day with no one to blame.
Plans and dreams are shattered and torn
Without a whisper or someone to forewarn.
Are you on a roller coaster of ups and downs
Waiting to get back to solid ground?
Little heartbreaks may occur, one by one
Don't let them turn into a marathon
Because a chain reaction is hard to stop
Like ripples in a lake when a pebble drops.
A domino effect may soon occur
As emotions run wild and cause a stir.
Instead, pray that hope will find a way
Chasing adversity to another day.
Like the earthy aroma of a running brook
Hope is humble, often hidden or overlooked.
If you remove bitterness and replace it with faith
God will make sure that little drops of hope remain.

A Reassuring Presence

Every day is another day to say thank you
For all the helpful things you faithfully do.
When I wake to see a smile on your face
It is a reassuring presence bestowing a toasty embrace
An unwavering love through darkness into light
Shining like a steady glow always within sight.
Heroic actions form a pattern throughout the day
Reinforcing the relationship in an extraordinary way.
In the face of adversity, an unshakable bond is growing
Stronger and without the outside world knowing
An unexpected benefit when living in troubling times
Finding hope in a web of complicated new designs.
God serves as a warm blanket of comfort at each day's start
Forming a shield of protection so you won't fall apart.
Worry has no place when faith remains in the air
Along with a reassuring presence of tender loving care.

Stillness and Tranquility

When searching for answers you need to be still
Don't take a vitamin supplement or a sleeping pill.
In moments of uncertainty you want to shut down
Or act like a hamster on a wheel going round-and-round
Running in circles wanting to pull out your hair
Restlessly bouncing between anxiety and despair.
This can result in irrational behavior and periods of stress
When you're unable to solve problems and feel like a mess.
It is important to fix your mind on what matters
Not trivial things that leave your heart in tatters.
Don't get overwhelmed by trying to do too much
Using non-stop activity as an emotional crutch.
Without tranquility you lack stability and genuineness—
Stillness is a discipline that takes continual practice
It sharpens your senses to rely more on God's presence
When you step away from the see-saw you're on
You'll finally sense the effervescence
Of a life with less anxiousness and worry
With God as the protagonist of your story.

A Healing Forecast

When you get sick and pain comes to visit
There are many emotions that it can elicit.
Even if diagnosed as just a cold or the flu
You need a prognosis to know what to do.

When a hurricane is imminent, you have to prepare
If your health is in jeopardy, you need extra care.
It may not be the path you had planned to take
Because you were sidetracked by an unfortunate break.

A detour like this may take you by surprise
Finding the best road to recovery becomes very wise.
You may have to change focus to weather the storm
Readjust and muster up strength in order to conform.

You will overcome waves of uncertainty
Knowing that God is in control for all of eternity.
When someone in your life has unconditional love for you
Nothing is impossible for a healing forecast to come true.

Picture Perfect

CHAPTER 3

Picture Perfect

When someone takes a photo of you
You immediately look to take a view
Wishing it to be idyllic like in a story book
Often you are disappointed at how you look.
You see flaws you didn't know you had
You question if you always look this sad
Wanting to appear happier, beautiful and rested
Not exactly how you see your vision reflected.
No one person is picture perfect at every moment
Outward beauty is not the only component
No one thing in this world is completely flawless
Before posting photos try to be very cautious.
Your inner charisma is what counts at the end of the day
And how you show it in what you do and say
With a giving nature and a humble heart
An aura of something special sets you apart.
By giving yourself a spiritual manicure
A refreshed and renewed magnificence occurs
In your natural body and in your spirit
Because God's presence is obviously inherent.

Shrinking

Without rain, the lake is shrinking
What must the birds and ducks be thinking?
They know that God will keep them safe
He always has in every case.

Is our respect for life shrinking
Without really any serious thinking?
If we don't hear or know the truth
Our perception and reality is in dispute.

If I don't agree, am I the enemy
Or does it reveal your real identity?
Our life span is shrinking I just read
One more thing to fear and dread.

God's love will never shrink away
If you ask Him to come and stay.
He stays constant, never changing
So why do we keep rearranging?

In the Blink of An Eye

Embrace every moment while you can
No one knows the length of each life span.
Things may change on a dime or in the blink of an eye
Situations can happen leaving you to wonder why.
When you hesitate and put something off to another day
You might not get another chance so think before you delay.
Be aware and ready because this could be your finest hour
Your place in time to shine with amazing strength and power.
There is a reason you are alive at this defining moment
You could easily come face to face with an unworthy opponent
Forcing the unthinkable and unexpected to happen
It can creep up on you as your world starts to blacken
As imperceptible events start to occur all around
Then in the blink of an eye the final trumpet will sound.
So now is the time to remove all timidity and fear
Spreading words of encouragement to all who will hear.

True Love

True love is infinite and eternal
There is no map, GPS, or journal.
It must be experienced first hand
In order to learn and understand.

Love doesn't happen right away
But grows stronger day by day.
True love is unselfish and kind
Embellishing the heart and mind.

Like the sea and sky, it is endless
A desire for solidarity that is relentless.
Deep and abiding love is resistant
To emotional whims and insistence.

It is a steadfast commitment and choice
One that doesn't always cause you to rejoice
When unforeseen circumstances and challenges
Upset its fluidity tipping the scale that balances.

Love involves perpetual devotion to one person
Giving and receiving it without control or coercion
Yielding completely, surrendering your heart
To honor the vows and promises made never to part.

Friend of a Wounded Heart

Is a friend of a wounded heart
Someone with a heart that also fell apart
And is still suffering from the break
With a few open wounds at stake?
How can they be a friend of a heart,
A delicate flower looking for a new start
Or a leaf in the wind restless and unrefined?
Only God knows where you are at this time
Understands the depth of your wounds
With the perfect cure to offer and include.
I think Jesus is your heart's true friend
He knows when the pains will end
Because only He can heal your silent scars
Mend your heart left unlatched and ajar.
If He dwells within your heart, it's guaranteed
That Jesus will supply all the love you need.

A Perfect Love

No matter what you're going through
His perfect love is there for you.
The chains that were binding are gone
You are forgiven, set free, no longer forlorn.
God has opened many doors
Picked you up off the floor
Performed miracles to keep you safe
Always there to help in every case.

When you call upon Him to lift you up
He comes along to fill your cup
With kind and loving affection
He provided a shield of protection
Even when you did not believe
He loved and taught you how to achieve
By gently nudging and calling your name
Until you were ready to join the game.

When you felt down and were shaken
He rescued you, there is no mistaking
He surrounded you each day and night
With a perfect love not always in plain sight.

Everyone wishes for a life of all blue skies
Until you eventually realize there are lies
Heard and felt by the world in which you live.
Don't place your hope in things that can't give
You a complete, pure and perfect love
That shines down upon you from above.

The Mirror of Perfection

When you look in the mirror and see your reflection
Are you hoping it will show absolute perfection?
But then you start to see all your flaws
Is this a trick to make you fall
Short of what you hoped to see
Not measuring up to who you want to be?

At everything, you want to be the very best
Staying in competition with all the rest.
You want to fit into the perfect mold
Realizing this is unattainable as you grow old.

Letting go of this impossible goal
Doesn't mean that you have to lose control.
Some people compensate by sheer exaggeration
With enhancements beyond the normal imagination
Showcasing a perfect scenario on social media
So popular that their bio might be found on Wikipedia.

The mirror of perfection can turn you into a fool
Disguising the truth is one of its tricks used as a tool
Telling you that you will be loved by everyone
And your life will be filled with all joy and fun.

If you continue to aim for perfection
It will lead to an unfortunate misconception.
It isn't possible to always be happy and problem free
As many things don't turn out as you hoped they would be.

When the pursuit of perfection is replaced by faith it is a relief
Because God will step in with direction and love beyond belief.

Mack and Cheese

CHAPTER 4

Mack and Cheese

Mack is the name of our dog
Sometimes he eats like a hog
If you give him a treat
His life is complete.

Our cat's name is Cheese
She is sometimes hard to please
Cheese has fluffy yellow-gold fur
If you scratch her chin she will purr.

Mack comes running when he is called
Cheese looks all around then will crawl
Mack accepts that you are the boss
Cheese is oblivious and at a loss.

You can always find hope in Mack's eyes
Cheese is mysterious and questions why
Mack is loyal and obedient
Cheese is mischievous and deviant.

Mack has useful fetching skills
Protector of the family is a job he fulfills
Tilts his head when he understands
He is part of our family's daily plans.

Cheese has beauty and grace
She loves napping in her special place
When she purrs it creates a comforting sound
Life is better with her around.

Mack and Cheese are different but live together
For them, getting along is a worthy endeavor
They love, forgive and have learned to live side by side
So why can't we do the same and put aside our pride?

The Little Bird and the Big Fish

Your eyes are bigger than your tummy
Is sometimes said when you picture food tasting so yummy
That you help yourself to more than you can ever eat.
When a little bird catches a big fish, it is difficult for the fish to compete

Because if a fish is bigger or the same size as the bird
The result is a scene that becomes very absurd.
As the little bird realizes, a big fish when caught will flop all around
And no matter how he maneuvers it, the fish is not going down.

Is it because the bird's eyes were bigger than his stomach
Or due to the flailing fish's dumb luck?
Probably bad luck for the fish because the bird has a stomach with 2 chambers.
In nature and life there are no guarantees or disclaimers.

A fish-eating bird has a very specialized digestive system
To help digest a whole fish using his natural wisdom.
The bird must orient the fish headfirst when swallowing it
In case the fish's fins expand when the bird tries to make it fit

Avoiding injury to his esophagus on the way down.
Did this little bird bite off more than it can chew with the fish it found
As he tried to achieve a feat very difficult for a bird like him
Grabbing more dinner than is enough with greed from within?

From this story, we learn that unlike a bird if we trust in the Lord
We will have all we need so that our future is ensured.
If we ask, we will receive all of our heart's desires
Without wastefulness we have all that life requires.

Magpies and Pie

A magpie is a bird famous for being a hoarder
You may not know this fact if you're not a birder.
They pick up almost anything they can easily haul
Known to ruin a golf game by hopping away with the ball!

They wouldn't be very popular in a golfing community
Chasing after a magpie could unhinge your credibility.
Magpies are considered to be intelligent creatures
Singing beautiful songs is one of their well-known features.

There are superstitions about magpies and their eating habits
They are omnivorous eating plants, seeds and sometimes rabbits.
Encountering one of these distinctive black-and-white birds
Can herald bad luck that can't be explained with words.

However, in some cultures they are considered sacred
Bringing happiness so its poor reputation is negated.
Somehow "magpie" became a word for a baked good
A pastry-filled crust that was often misunderstood.

It was later shortened to just "pie"
Which seems quite ambiguous as to why.
So the next time you're enjoying a nice piece of pie
Think of a magpie flying high in the sky.

Will Curiosity Kill the Cat?

Curiosity killed the cat
But satisfaction brought it back.

The first line of this simple idiom is warning you
That being overly curious can bring disorder into view.
It is an expression used when someone asks prying questions
Trying to find out something without good intentions
When it is none of their business
And not eligible for forgiveness.

The second line is often forgotten
Leaving the cat feeling misbegotten.
But it really does alter the meaning
Making the full idiom less demeaning
Especially to the cat!
Because curiosity can't really kill a cat just like that.

So isn't it good news to know the cat is alive
It won't take a dive and is going to survive?
The moral is to be careful when being too nosey
Or you might create a situation that is not very rosy.
So if you don't fall prey to gossip and heed the warning
Curiosity won't kill the cat and you'll be glad in the morning.

The Gator Who Lived Next Door

Although Ali, the gator, lives in a lake
It really is not a terrible mistake
To consider him as a neighbor
Even though most people won't give him the favor.

Every day he smoothly glides by before dark
Always looking for some place to park
With his head peeking out above the water
To show that he's an expert explorer
Looking for something to eat
As birds try not to be his next treat.

So how do I know he's not a crocodile
If you try to guess it might take awhile.
Crocodiles have a wider snout
That is really not so easy to spot.
They are darker in color with overlapping jaws
Which often makes you stop and pause.

Most people think that alligators have no purpose
But there is more to them than what's on the surface.
In the ecosystem, they play an important role
Through the creation of alligator holes
That provide both wet and dry habitats
Where other organisms live and will thrive in fact.

All living creatures interact in various ways
As seen in the splendor that the earth displays.
Ali, the gator, who lives next door is not a threat
As long as he is not treated as a pet.

Don't Tell Me
I Can't Dance Anymore

CHAPTER 5

Don't Tell Me I Can't Dance Anymore

Without dance I might lose my mind
Act crazy, become lazy or be unkind.
Dancing eases worry about problems I face
Taking away heartaches that are hard to erase.

Please don't tell me I have to stop
You know I'm always going to dance until I drop.
Put on my dancing shoes as my feet take flight
If I couldn't dance it would be a dreadful plight!

So I will jump out of my chair
And dance like I really don't care
Being active and feeling alive
Shuffling to the music as other dancers jive.

I'll be on the dance floor until the music ends
Moving to the beat as it starts to blend
Getting euphoric so I can forget for a while.
It's better than seeing a shrink; not my style.

Please don't say I'm getting too old
Because when dancing I am very bold.
I don't expect to win any awards
Just want to have fun and be restored.

Can You Dance in Heaven?

Can you dance in heaven
One dance after another in succession
More beautifully than ever before
Can you dance for evermore?

Can you dance without stopping
Never feeling tired or worried of dropping
No aches, pains or soreness do you feel
You can even click your heels?

In heaven, can you float on a cloud
While singing a song clear and loud
Sounding like church bells chiming
Melodic harmony in perfect timing?

There is no room for pain or fear
No sounds of hate will you hear.
There's no sadness or tears to cry
You do not have to wonder why.

On earth something is missing
There's no time for reminiscing.
Something is really not quite right
You must have left you're no where in sight.

Lost in the Dance

If the sting of heartbreak and its cost
Reminds you of a love that was lost
Just get lost in the dance
As the music sings of new romance.

Stowing thoughts of what you once had
Floating away whether good or bad
Love changed and it had to end
Now your heart has to mend.

Once tenderly loved and caressed
As your love was gently expressed
Sensations felt now only in a dream
Or when trying to catch a moonbeam.

A dance will entwine you in its beat
Erasing that sense of longing and defeat
Love shifted and was not the same
With no one to claim the blame.

As the rhythm of the music begins to flow
Your heart swells and is all aglow
The dance takes on a new meaning
Your senses come alive and are beaming.

Suddenly you're lost in the dance
Ready to risk it all and take a chance
With each step your heart heals a little more
As it looks forward to what's in store.

Your light has been restored
No matter what went on before
Refreshed, renewed, enhanced
Forever lost in the dance.

Dancers and Drummers

One dancer, two dancers, three dancers, four
In a minute there will be more out on the floor
Five, six, seven dancers and maybe more
So many keep joining it's hard to be sure.

As different songs are played by choice or chance
Dancers out on the floor seem to know the dance
Whether it is in a ballroom, a home or even outdoors
They dance to patterns of steps set to musical scores.

One drummer, two drummers, three drummers, four
Setting up their buckets and balls on the floor
Soon the room is filled with lots of drummers drumming
Moving and singing along as the atmosphere is humming.

Cardio drumming may be new to you
But it is worth a try to see it through
It can't help but lift your spirits and mood
Having fun while exercising is what you'll conclude.

So how many dancers dancing can you count on the floor
At any given time there may be less or more?
Counting drummers might be easier to do
Because once set up and ready they usually don't move.

Drummers drumming, dancers dancing what can go wrong
Doesn't this sound like part of the "Twelve Days of Christmas" song?
If you look around and see a partridge in a pear tree
They may have to change the song if you spot two or three.

The Little Things

All too often we take the little things in life for granted
Never showing appreciation before becoming disenchanted.
Happiness shouldn't be measured in material possessions
This kind of attitude can quickly turn into maniacal obsessions.

Why not focus on the little things that money can't buy?
For example, the sun as it shines brightly against a blue sky
Or a grandchild's hug, their giggle and beautiful smile
Playing a game, reading a book and relaxing for awhile.

When a promise is kept or a sincere compliment given
You see that all these little things make life worth living.
A walk on the beach, a refreshing swim, dodging the waves
The possibilities that a new baby brings when a life is saved.

A dance, a song being sung and a friendly gesture
Are all priceless instances that add love and adventure.
When someone calls who you were just thinking about
It is a special surprise that you don't want to live without.

As you continue you can't help but discover there are so many more
Like praying for someone who has never been prayed for before.
You will soon find these little things are too numerous to count
We encounter God's blessings every day there is no doubt.

A Safety Net

CHAPTER 6

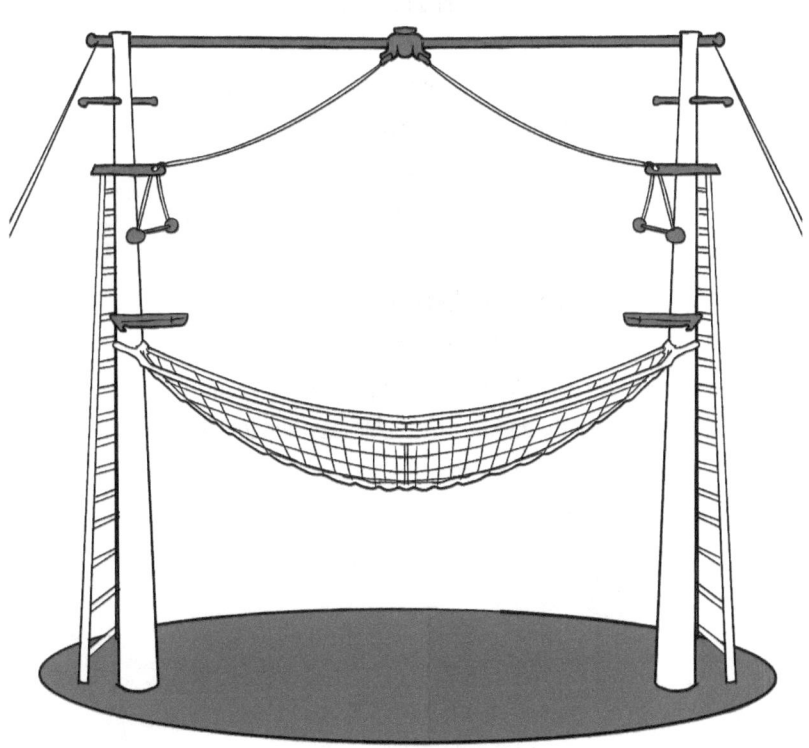

A Safety Net

Do you have a net that will catch you if you fall
With a plan that doesn't include building a wall
What serves as your refuge, your place of safety
To rescue you in times of trouble and frailty?
God promises to help you to avoid the traps
That can crush and cause you to collapse.
Too many people don't stop to think
About having a safe haven so they do not sink
Deep into helplessness and mental fatigue
Where they find deception and unhealthy intrigue.
Your body and mind need a place of escape
To pray, summarize your next steps, and reshape.
Don't worry about what everyone else is doing
You are only in charge of what you are pursuing.
Learn to think for yourself when making decisions
Never waffle back and forth with too many revisions.
Fearing people is a dangerous trap
But trusting the Lord will close the gap
Between what is wrong and what is right
He will rescue and protect you with His light
From the darkness of trouble, pain and threats
With His unbreakable safety nets
To make it easier to face and handle every situation
Knowing that the final reward is your salvation.

Gifts, Talents, and Passions

God has placed you where you are for a reason
He has given you gifts, talents, and a passion.
Often they are discovered and employed at an early age
Or may lie dormant and are realized at a later stage.
Either way it is important to help those around you
Displaying God's glory in everything you say and do.
Whether it's when socializing, working or just staying home
Be energized and innovative in the seeds that you have sown,
Bringing hope to those struggling with a hard decision
Or who are facing a difficult life situation.
Your uniqueness sets the stage to apply new-found talents
While still maintaining a natural spiritual balance.
You were born with a package of capabilities
To be unwrapped and used at various opportunities.
Deep in the heart of every person is a desire to make a difference,
A longing for a chance to be a reflection of God's magnificence.
By finding your purpose and understanding your value
Anything is possible when a dream comes into view.

Nuggets of Friendship

• Friendships are born in a million different ways
It's a gift to find a friend that is loyal and never strays.
• All good friends strive to achieve the same goal
To be a source of love and support
But only a few become part of your soul.
• Finding a true friend feels like a gift
That keeps on giving even when there's a rift.
A listening ear, a shoulder to cry on
Someone you can always rely on.
• True friends are never apart
Maybe in distance but never in heart.
• A friend is one who overlooks your broken fence
But admires the flowers in your garden without pretense.
• A true friend is a rainbow in your cloud
Always bright and uplifting but never too proud.
• In the cookie of life, friends are the chocolate chips
Adding something unique and special like a solar eclipse.
• Many people will walk into your life, then depart
But only a true friend will leave footprints on your heart.
• Good friends are like stars, you may not always see

But you always feel their presence to some degree.
• A true friend is like a four-leaf clover, hard to find
But lucky to have and always so kind.
• There's nothing like really loyal dependable friends
Because nothing can replace them; a perfect blend.
• Awards become corroded and may even rust
A friend gathers no dust and is someone you trust.
• A good friend will always try to lift you higher
Never put you down just give what you require.
• Friends are those rare people who ask how you are
Then wait to hear the answer from near or far.
• A friend knows the song that is in your heart
And sings it to you if your memory suddenly falls apart.
• Great friends are hard to find, difficult to leave,
Impossible to forget but always easy to believe.
• Friendship is the golden thread that ties the heart of all the world
Added to love and respect will cause harmony to be unfurled.

Solving Life's Equation

Something seems to be missing in today's life equation.
Everyone tries to make it on their own with little emotion.
Feelings are easily hurt, loneliness and frustrations abound.
While searching for hope, hearts are broken, no love to be found.
Today's life equation appears to focus on Me, Me, Me and Now, Now, Now
Substituting factors like empathy and compassion; can we figure out how?
Is there a common denominator or are we really this shallow?
Many lives lack depth, offer no fulfillment, and are infinitely hollow.
Protests and riots never really solve the original problem
They don't offer a solution or produce any sense of satisfaction.
Isn't it better to initiate change through constructive and positive action?
Lacking respect for opposing viewpoints and honor for the dignity of life
Will only lead to misery and create pain, discomfort and strife.
The passcode to happiness is lost in the shuffle.
The exponent involved comes across as hustle and bustle.
An eraser is needed before the current equation can be solved
Start over, be open to new possibilities so problems are resolved.
A new-found life equation can reset the old pattern so all can live free.
Substituting love for hate ensures that each life has renewed jubilee.
As a result, the new equation will be simple to understand and easy to see:
(You + God + Jesus + Love) − (hatred + evil) = peace for all eternity.

Your Internal Dialogue

A little voice inside tries to tell you how you should be feeling
Giving signals to help improve your health and well-being.
This internal dialog may be saying not to be so serious
To let loose, laughing out loud until you're happily delirious.
If you relax a little while each day
Peace will come and want to stay.
Don't listen to sounds of doubt and negativity
It will only reduce your level of productivity.
Look inside, dig deep to overcome the fear
So your internal dialogue becomes very clear.
Listen to the voice inside your head
Not the world's advice that creates unnecessary dread.
Learn how to tune into the frequency of your inner voice
So that you can analyze and make a wise choice
Allowing you to focus on only positive thoughts
And not be influenced by questionable naughts.
A quiet whisper will warn you of any possible downsides
To avoid rushing into something that is unwise.
Aim for balance between your mind and heart
Fill them with sincere gratitude as the major part
Bringing you back to where there is purity of perception
As God's presence covers you with His divine protection.

Lollygagging

Kids often lollygag before making a decision
Aimlessly wasting time especially with no supervision.
It is a funny and unusual word
Along with many others you may have already heard.
Hopscotching is another unusual one
Meaning skipping from place to place and having fun
Moving kind of erratically
Not very systematically.
Tiptoeing occurs when someone walks quietly and carefully
Raising their heels temporarily
With the weight on the balls of their feet
Trying to be very quiet and discreet.
Or it can mean to carefully avoid a sensitive subject
Worried that someone might get offended and object.
A ragamuffin refers to a ragged and often disreputable person
It also is a breed of cat but I am not really certain.
Rigamarole means to be confused by all the red tape
Like what's involved when your health is at stake.
A pettifogger is a nitpicker who quibbles over trifles
Worrying about the difference between dashes and hyphens.

It is also the name given to shrewd lawyers
Mentioned in jokes to make their image seem smaller.
Bailiwick is a sphere in which someone has superior knowledge
And usually is an authority on a subject like a scholar.
A boondoggle is a wasteful or impractical project
That in other words becomes a pain in your neck.
Bumbershoot is a slang word for umbrella
Forget it in rainy weather and you could face a dilemma.
Cattywampus means something is off-kilter or askew
When you look out the window and don't like the view.
A barnburner is an event that is extremely interesting or exciting
Like a special concert when there are several rock star sightings.
Crestfallen is a feeling of shame, humiliation or dejection
Like if a team loses the playoff game, they may face rejection.

You probably can think of many more
Try naming a few, there is no keeping score.
If you play Wordle or Scrabble it could help you do better
So you can be the next word-game trendsetter.

Hanging Just By A Thread

CHAPTER 7

Just By a Thread

"Their confidence hangs by a thread.
They are leaning on a spider's web."
Job 8:14 describes what a dangerous situation
It is to be hanging by a thread
Not sure how lightly you need to tread.
A minor alteration can change the outcome
Stay steady and strong so as not to succumb.
If you are hanging by a thread in a relationship
You may soon be receiving a pink slip
With not much hope of it ever surviving
So just forget about any high five-ing.
When a button is attached by one single thread or strand
You're bound to lose it and never know where it might land.
In social media, a string of messages making up a conversation
Creates a new and effective way of communication
Called a thread that begins with an initial message or text
And continues as a series of replies not overly complex.
This type of thread includes family members or friends
To help stay informed and follow the latest trends.

It shouldn't replace a personal phone call
Even though a thread keeps track for easy recall.
Sometimes this may initiate a texting firestorm
Of multiple back-and-forth responses that form
Until your head starts to spin
And there's no way to win.
So it's a good idea to set your phone to silent mode
Especially when sleeping so it doesn't explode.
Also using talk-to-text can induce some mysticism
When an incorrect word appears causing skepticism.

Our lives hang just by a thread
Whenever we venture out into the world.
God watches over us as each day occurs
Knowing how the threads of our lives intertwine.
It is all part of His plan and design.

Consistency

Consistency is the basis of trust
Keeping your promises is a must
To establish a pattern of reliability
Always do good things often and repetitively.
When you are consistent, people trust and respect you
They never question that what you say is not true.
Devotion and dedication are part of the consistency package
Bumps in the road will shake away any unnecessary baggage.
Consistency can make raindrops that fall create holes in a rock
Persistence and perseverance work together like a fine-tuned clock.
Consistency is the path that leads to accomplishment of a goal
Even if you fail a hundred times or more, eventually progress takes control.
Your purpose is clearer and a breakthrough is conceivable
When all things become possible, success is achievable.
If you focus on what you want, God will clear the way
Because faithfulness and commitment are on display.

Triangulation

I heard the term triangulation used and wasn't sure what it meant.
One meaning is that it's a strategy that has a manipulative intent.
A devious method to control a situation in order to get one's way
That becomes a skillful game that seems to be played everyday.
It often becomes a chronic device used to pit people against one another
An underhanded technique that can be very hard to uncover.
I sometimes feel we are trapped when listening to the news.
Stories are selected or slanted so we hear only one point of view.
Journalists should always report the truth after careful study of the facts.
Readers or viewers hear a one-sided agenda presented to cause an impact.
Repeated over and over until the truth is lost and we start to believe
You have to wonder what is the main outcome they hope to achieve.
What happened to honest reporting so you trust in all that is said?
You may have to check other sources and do your own research instead.
The news media and what is released should be taken with a grain of salt.
Check various sources, be on the lookout for anything that causes you to halt.
Why not try prayer and meditation to suspend judgment of all that you hear?
Unleash natural curiosity, be aware, don't overreact, it won't eliminate the fear.
Avoid getting overwhelmed and distracted, focus only on what you can control.
Have confidence and faith in God to provide hope for the future as a worthy goal.

Life's Instruction Book of Wisdom

You don't have to spend money on the latest self-help book
Just open your Bible to Proverbs and take a look.
You'll find practical advice infused with divine wisdom
Capsules of truth to help develop a daily plan and system.
There is guidance to help solve problems and everyday dilemmas
Words of discernment to reduce failures and increase successes.
Each proverb offers simple instruction for every situation we face.
That inspires reverence and obedience we can't easily erase.
Written to improve alertness and discretion in all of our tasks
That cultivates keenness of mind to remove our disguises or masks.
Regardless of our differences that sometimes divide us
As human beings we are united by much the same challenges.
The sensible counsel of proverbs applies to all people in all places
Throughout time and in all cultures and earthly spaces.
Knowing and doing right along with common sense
Keeps you safe from disaster and on the right path.
God wrote the book giving mercy and grace for all who ask
Leading towards a relationship with Him that if nurtured will last.
An honest and pure faith that establishes a foundation of well-being
Ensures a life of peace, joy, and fulfillment when God is intervening.

Blind Insensitivity

We encounter all types of people as part of life's design
Some add a unique value that helps us to realign
Challenging and encouraging us to be better
A beneficial effect not easy to measure.
Many people are negative and blindly insensitive
They often are unusually emotional and argumentative.
Their bites and barbs often seem mean
And may erode our self-esteem.
Sometimes people are too involved in their own narrative
To have concern for anyone else's perspective.
Don't react in kind; they may be facing troubled times.
Show compassion even, if to you, it may seem benign.
You don't know what someone is going through
A kind word or action can turn their skies to blue.
Beautiful and gracious words will stir their hearts
Creating a climate of harmony and amity to start.
Erasing an environment of blind insensitivity in which we live
Begins by being thankful in all circumstances and willing to forgive.

Hanging Onto High Hopes

You are the wind behind my sails
Because your love never fails
We can construct a boat
To help us stay afloat.

So if the water starts to rise
You will be there by my side
If we have each other that is all we need
With God showing us how to proceed.

When there is a desire for a brighter day
It washes away whatever gets in the way
God lives within our hearts and mind
So nothing can touch us that is unkind.

A strong faith is what wins this game
Hanging on to high hopes for a change
In course that leads to smoother sailing
Erasing away dark clouds from trailing.

A Bright Crescent Moon

CHAPTER 8

A Crescent Moon

Looking up at the night sky you observe a sliver of light
Each evening it grows larger becoming an iconic sight
Like a prayer slowly answered, hope sets in and abounds
The phenomenon unfolding on a dark sky is quite profound.
Stages of the crescent moon can have a spiritual meaning
The waning and waxing phases represent two paths intervening
Before or after the new moon becomes full and bright
Is a time to focus and renew your resolve each night.
The waxing moon is visible because of the sun's reflection
Creating a pattern of light that is sheer perfection
As the moon continues its orbit around the earth
You may experience a sense of renewal and rebirth.
The reflection begins again to take on a crescent shape
The waning moon's spiritual meaning is one of escape
A chance to let go of anything that is no longer purposeful
And cling to all the things in your life that are worshipful.
God created the full moon so we will look up, ponder and gaze
Knowing that life's darkest times soon become brighter days.

A Healing Forecast

When you get sick and pain comes to visit
There are many emotions that it can elicit.
Even if diagnosed as just a cold or the flu
You need a prognosis to know what to do.
When a hurricane is imminent, you have to prepare
If your health is in jeopardy, you need extra care.
It may not be the path you had planned to take
Because you were sidetracked by an unfortunate break.
A detour like this may take you by surprise
Finding the best road to recovery becomes very wise.
You may have to change focus to weather the storm
Readjust and muster up strength in order to conform.
You will overcome waves of uncertainty
Knowing that God is in control for all of eternity.
When someone in your life has unconditional love for you
Nothing is impossible for a healing forecast to come true.

Standing on the Outside

Sometimes I feel like I'm standing on the outside
Looking into a scene where I'm trying to hide.
A montage of my life is being shown from afar
Then I realize it is me who is the star.
Like a dream, it feels like I will wake soon
Before the sun rises and I see the moon.
At times, we all feel a little lost
Not sure we can keep paying the cost.
Heartaches are often too hard to bear
Setbacks don't always seem to be fair.
Suddenly we realize that nothing compares
To the sound of Your voice heard in our prayers
Showering us with comfort, shelter, and love
Prepared for us by powers from above.
You fill us with hope with each passing day
Not allowing trivial thoughts to get in the way
Of giving thanks for the blessings we are given
And for our sins that have been forgiven.
Filling the emptiness we were feeling inside
With the knowledge that You will be our guide.
Life isn't perfect but with the sound of Your name
We can step out of the darkness without any shame
No longer on the outside when You intercept
Because promises made are promises kept.

The Selective Listening Technique

Do you ever feel like no one listens to you
Never wanting to hear your point of view?
They say they are too busy to chat
And have to go home to feed the cat.
Excuses excuses, I have heard them all
I didn't hear the phone and missed your call.
Maybe its because they have wax in their ears
And not due for a check up until later this year.
They keep saying you don't talk loud enough
Making good communication really so tough.
Other reasons and excuses they might give—
I forgot to wear my hearing aids, please forgive.
So you try with all your might to shout it so loud
That the angels hear it way up in the clouds.
When you're in another room where the TV is blasting
And your stomach is growling because you are fasting,
It is understandable that you can't really be heard
But at some point the situation becomes quite absurd.
Could this be implementation of their selective listening technique
Or should we chalk it up as part of our feminine mystique?

Jars of Clay

CHAPTER 9

Jars of Clay

After a simple piece of clay is shaped,
Bent and molded into a jar and baked
It sometimes will crack and break just like us.
Living in the environment of today, we have to adjust
To the ways of the world and not be battered
Like a clay jar that is so easily broken or shattered.
Society relays misconceptions about who we are
Often feeling alone, not worthy or special like a star.
We are told to look and act in a certain way
But we are uniquely made no matter what they say.
God is the Potter, Artist and Creator of our story
Ultimately, we are all used by God for His glory
Molding us in different ways just like a jar of clay.
Our light shines through the cracks in exceptional ways
Out into the world to share the treasures of our heart
That leads to salvation and a fresh perspective about to start.

Just Like That—A Prayer

Just like that—a prayer is answered
Not a prayer considered standard
But one you thought was out of sight
Wishing with all your heart that it might.
Maybe you said a prayer a long time ago
Kept the faith because you wanted it so
Almost giving up but you kept asking
Knowing God's promises are everlasting.
God hears you the first time you pray
His timing is always wise even with a delay
You will see why and then understand
It's on a perfect timetable and master plan.
Miracles are possible when God is in control
If you wait patiently the result will console
Whenever you start to think God is being silent,
Behind the scenes He's working to be compliant.
Stay calm, have faith, the answer is on its way—
Blessed and assured that everything will be okay.

"Needle in a Haystack"

When looking for a needle in a haystack
Leave no stone unturned and don't look back.
You might have to turn a place upside down
And inside out to search and look all around.
You may even have to go on a wild goose chase
Lose your dignity spending time you can't replace.
It will be something that is not so difficult to find
When you start to believe you are one of a kind.
You will realize the needle in the haystack is YOU
Discovering how unique you are and believing it's true.
As you crawl out of the haystack a light begins to shine
With a reflection that sparkles, radiating a redesign—
A refined purpose with a newfound passion to embrace
Enjoying an enhanced sense of satisfaction taking place.
You are a needle in today's haystack that stands out
Through belief and a power that takes root and sprouts
To improve the lives of others and find fulfillment
Living without adversity to become stable and resilient
Reaching out to the lost who are left with despair
Showing them how to look closely and be aware
That a sacred and revered needle is within sight
Helping them out of the darkness and into the light.
You are the needle in the haystack of everyday life
Who was found and saved from struggle and strife.
God is the everlasting needle in today's haystack world
An Oyster encasing the only pure and eternal Pearl.

FEB 9 1926 - DEC 3 2013

The Dash Between the Dates

The time between our birth and death is a gift
The gift is life and the period of time that we exist.
The dash between the dates indicates life's fleeting nature—
Its span being controlled by our creator.
What we do with it gives our life meaning
With values and inherent feelings intervening.
Love and relationships form a major part of the dash
Remembered more than possessions that do not last.
The choices we make dictate the dash's fiber and texture
How it all comes together we can only conjecture.
Decisions we arrive at weave into our life's tapestry.
A synergy occurs slowly at first and with time more rapidly.
There are many ways it becomes enriched in depth and quality
Starting with our life's pattern of benevolence and generosity.
The dash includes our faith, convictions, and belief system
Along with a background of genuine love and infinite wisdom.
We all desire for our life to remain significant to friends and family
By leaving behind an invaluable legacy to ensure our immortality.
Stains and blemishes cannot be erased from the fabric of our past
However, we can begin sowing seeds of positivity that will last.

Light, Laughter, and Love

Always move slowly toward the light
So when the sun disappears into the night
You are assured it will rise again tomorrow
With a renewed purpose in which to follow.
A sunrise can boost your emotional state
After a full moon lights up the sky when it is late.
Try to move away from the darkness
Although clouds will appear regardless.
Doubt is seen as darkness in your eyes
Whereas uncertainty can be easily disguised.
It is like fog or a heavy mist
Blocking the sun even though it still exists.
The mist is sometimes thick and heavy like a blanket
A weather pattern not suited for an outside banquet.
Thunder involves a dark sky that brings loud rumblings
As lightning streaks through cloud-like dumplings.
Love grows in the light of the sun
It brings laughter and unexpected fun.

A spontaneous laugh is like soup boiling over
It spreads joy like a walk in a field of grass and clover.
Laughter is considered the music of the soul
It can make you lose control.
Laughter is a perfect mood enhancer
Similar to a whimsical song and rhythmic dancer.
Love and laughter will smooth off the edges
So you don't fear walking on narrow ledges.
Love gives you strength to try once more
Helping you to get your boat to shore.
Love grows when hatred stops spreading
Looking forward to the future instead of dreading.
Love shows the world that the best is yet to come
When you believe that God's work has just begun.
Light and laughter helps you to make it through
But nothing else compares to God's love for you.

The Ultimate Antidote

Why worry and fret over things you can't control
Allowing anxiety and stress to take its toll
Like a ball of yarn when it comes unwound
Not able to stop it from rolling all around?
Worry impedes boldness, energy and focus
Creating instances that cause neurosis
Crushing your spirit tossing you to and fro
As you stand waiting for the sun to show.
It's similar to being out in stormy weather
Looking for a wave of calm acting as a tether
To anchor you and cast out antagonistic emotions
Preventing any additional spiritual erosion.
A sense of tranquility forms within your heart
When destructive habits fall apart.
There is hope and comfort to be found
That lifts your mood helping to rebound.
We can dance, sing and be ready to perform
Or just take a long nap to help calm the storm.
But the most effective way to stay afloat
Is to let Christ be the ultimate antidote.

Sea Monsters
and Other Scary Things

CHAPTER 10

The Sinister Sea Monster

The sea monster can be sinister and insensitive
His demeanor and vibe is wicked and negative.
He lurks and hangs around so it is hard to break free
You want him to leave you alone and go back to the sea.
He is slippery and sly making waves that rock your boat
Clouding your mind when you're trying to stay afloat.
He has an ominous nature when he gets out of control
You have to convince him to stop this pessimistic flow.
Slimy and scaly spouting jets of foul water,
He's an unsinkable sea serpent, ruffian and marauder.
He circles around waiting for an opportune moment to emerge
You need to find a way to get him to permanently submerge.
Chasing him away with some clever and devious schemes
A dream catcher can be hung to trap your bad dreams.
Prayers too will help remove any evil spirits still lurking
And to ensure that your efforts are working
So he'll go back to the sea without a chance of recall
With this sinister sea monster conquered once and for all.

What Good Is It?

What good is a checklist if you never check it
Not very useful you have to admit.
What good is a prayer if it is never prayed
Without prayer you may always be afraid.
What good is a thought if it is never expressed
It fades from memory and will never be assessed.
What good is a grocery list if you leave it at home
Up and down all the aisles you will have to roam.
What good is a phone call if it is never made
Like a song on the radio that is never played.
What good is a card if it is never sent
No one will know your true intent.
What good is a project that you never complete
You will gradually feel a sense of defeat.
What good is a book if it is never read
It just sits on the shelf or beside your bed.
What good is a promise that you do not keep
People may not trust you the next time you speak.
What good is love if you don't give it away
You may not have the chance on another day.

Heroes to Zeros

Where have all our heroes gone?
Heroes have always been held up as examples to follow
Expected to be super strong and not ever hollow.
Where's the magic that used to surround?
Removed from the spotlight, it no longer abounds.

A hero is someone admired for their steadfast courage.
Respected and looked up to at most every occurrence.
Throughout sports history, we held these athletes in high esteem.
Couldn't wait for their next game to cheer for our home team.

Forced now to hear their political opinions we don't care to know.
Noble qualities we looked up to, where did they go?
Fans are now saddened and sometimes feel ashamed.
Enjoyment and excitement can no longer be claimed.

Heroes become zeros when we watch them taking a knee.
As Americans this is not what we came here to see.
Can't they stand proudly with hands on their hearts?
When did this disrespect for our flag and country start?
Don't they realize they are alienating many of their fans?
God-given talents now wasted they hold right in their hands.

There exists only one true and perfect hero that we can appoint.
Our faith will lead us to Him and He will never disappoint.
He's our rock and our strength so we never will lose
A most divine and heavenly hero to have if we choose.

Battles and Blessings

Sometimes all I see are battles
So I stumble, fall and gravel
When victory should fill my mind
Leaving thoughts of defeat behind.

Sometimes all I see is the mountain
Rather than looking for a healing fountain
Trusting that the mountain can be moved
So circumstances can change and improve.

Sometimes all I see is a hard fight ahead
Not focusing on winning the battle instead.
I often feel all alone and do not see
Your love that is surrounding me.

Sometimes all I feel is fear
So I am unable to hear
Your voice when it says my name
Telling me I'm not to blame.

If we believe that battles can turn into blessings
We will begin to understand all of God's lessons
That help us to see things from a perspective bigger than ourselves
Equipping us to move forward with strength and spiritual wealth.

The Tongue is a Mighty Sword

Prayer is a powerful tool if you trust and believe.
All things are possible in God's time to achieve.

The tongue is a mighty sword that becomes a creative force.
Victory or defeat begins in the mind so what is your choice?
You probably have heard the saying what you say is what you get.
Thoughts are seeds planted in the garden of your mindset.
Words you speak can determine what direction your life will take.
It's really quite simple; you take control through words that you choose.
Negative thoughts and how you express them can cause you to lose.
What's conceived in your heart can hold you in unwanted bondage
Or shine brightly providing comfort and not be held hostage.

From beginning of time God said let there be light.
He spoke the world into existence as it came into sight.

So think before you speak and decide to hold back your tongue.
Positivity breeds positivity like verses of a hymn that is sung.

An act of kindness and a nice word can make someone's day.
The heartache they are feeling may all float away.
A storyteller can speak truth and lighten the way.

Corrupt communication is deceptive and hurtful as it repeats.
Fear prevents you from speaking victory and only defeats.

We all are human and make mistakes that set us on the wrong track
Uttering words that are hurtful then wishing you could take them all back.
Saying something unkind can create enemies of the people you hold dear
Family members don't speak to each for years causing so many tears.

God will forgive you with a humble request, He will always abide.
Tomorrow is a new day, turn a new leaf, it's up to you to decide.
Think carefully before speaking, use wisdom as your guide.
Optimistic remarks become beacons of hope and love you can't hide.

The Sock Monster

Where did that missing sock go
Will it always be a no-show?
What do you do with one purple sock
Or that pink one that went with that one special frock?

Is there a sock monster in your washer or dryer
Who steals and hides socks whenever it desires?
Is it stuck inside other clothes due to static cling
Did you leave it in a class or lose it at the gym?

Is it temporarily missing or never to be found
Even though you searched high and low and looked all around?
Maybe you left one inside your shoe or somewhere on the floor
Then kicked it under the bed or put it in the wrong drawer.

Sometimes we all misplace our glasses or phone
When our mind wonders into the twilight zone.
But with all the mathematical logic that the best minds have applied
We still don't know where that maniacal sock monster hides.

Happy Holidays

CHAPTER 11

Another Day or a Better Way

Today is the first day of a brand new year
Does it bring hope for the future or fill you with fear?
Is it really just another day
Or the beginning of a better way
To be thankful for the good times
Leaving the negative ones behind?
Do you have the courage to start over
Like a writer, poet, or musical composer
Stepping out of your comfort zone
But not wanting to do it all alone?
Suddenly, you get a glimpse into your future
That can't be found on a phone or computer.
But only in your mind do you see an array of possibilities
That take advantage of new or latent capabilities.
With each new year you can resolve to be braver
To change any undesirable trait or behavior,
Accomplish a new personal goal or improve one in play
By following a blueprint of love for a hope-filled brighter day.

Christmas Snow Globes

At Christmas time snow globes are frequently seen all around
Enclosing a miniaturized winter scene with snow falling down.
Snowmen, reindeer, Santa Claus, mistletoe or holly may appear
To show that Christmas is coming soon or is very near.
If there was a snow globe that depicts a happy scene from your life
A memory of a Christmas past, a day of joy without any strife
What would you choose
If there is nothing for you to lose?
Would it be a Christmas morning when you were a child
Waiting for Santa with anticipation that was hard to hide?
Perhaps a happy memory when you were first in love
Standing under mistletoe like a star-struck turtle dove?
Or a scene commemorating your baby's first Christmas morn
A delightful time when you lived each day for that little newborn?
This year many people are distraught because they feel so alone.
Their only contact with loved ones is by video or talking on the phone.
So try to picture a snow globe showcasing the newborn baby Jesus
Demonstrating God's love in a snow globe so we see the real reason
To promote healing and renewed strength throughout this season
His birth brought great joy into the world, a snow globe for all time.
The son of God arrives on earth providing hope and peace sublime.

Roses or Rosé

Which would you choose: red roses or a bottle of rose`
For your birthday or on Valentine's Day?
Roses are pretty and meant for someone special
Especially when carried in a fragile fanciful vessel.
When given to you from someone you love and cherish,
It is a gift that you will aesthetically relish.
On the other hand, a cold glass of rose` is soft like a kiss
That will impart a sweet, mellow feeling of bliss.
Opposite of the story line in the movie "War of the Roses"
Is a story with a happy ending with some romantic surprises
Where it doesn't matter if you receive flowers or wine
Because just being together makes every day seem fine
And the other person's happiness is more essential than your own.
Love is like the wind, you can't see but feel it when it's candidly shown.
To be fully seen by somebody else and be loved anyhow
Is the best gift you can have that only true love allows.

Irish and Stylish

I'm stylish
Because I am Irish.
Or am I Irish
Because I am stylish?
Anyway, on St. Patrick's Day:
I act in a very stylish/Irish way.
I wear shamrocks in my hair
And dance the Irish jig like I don't care.
I play Irish music on a harp
While waiting for the parade to start.
When the leprechauns march by I wave and cheer
While drinking a pint of green-colored beer.
I wear green before and on St. Patrick's Day
Whether you are Irish or not it's the Celtic way.
I wear a necklace with a Celtic knot
What the meaning is I have forgot
I think it represents water, earth, and fire
Or is it corned beef, cabbage and fancy attire?
My favorite Irish line dance is "Pot of Gold"
Dance it 100 times and you'll never grow old!

The Hare and the Egg

The Easter Bunny is known for delivering eggs and toys
On Easter morning to well-behaved girls and boys.
In American his name is Peter Cottontail.
However, in many cultures the Easter bunny is a female
Named Eostre after an Anglo-Saxon goddess
Who is associated with rejuvenation and promise.
Easter is celebrated on the Sunday after the first full moon
When we anticipate the resurrection that is approaching soon.
Eggs are symbols of life everlasting, fertility, potential, and hope.
The hare has become a sacred creature mythical in scope
Representing intuition and transformation.
Together, the hare and egg are a powerful representation
Of the glory of Spring with its budding grasses and warming light
Heralding the magnificent return of life to earth within our sight.

A Tribute to Dads on Father's Day

A Dad is an anchor, a leader, a guide
A steady hand in whom you can confide.
He is the rock and cornerstone of the family
Even if faced with situations he does not foresee.
His love is unshakable and unconditional
Not perfect but his dedication is unequivocal.
"Obey" is a word that is often misused
Replace it with "respect" so not misconstrued.
Without a father, the family balance is unstable
His role is to be strict but fair, strong yet gentle.
Although helpful and kind, he does make mistakes
But learns from them knowing what's at stake.
He treats the family as an inseparable unit
If there is a problem he works to get through it.
You might be saying, this doesn't describe the Dad I had
Anyone can be a father but not necessarily a good Dad.
It is unfortunate but rise above it, be a beacon for change
Learn from the past to help to change and rearrange
The future where a father is respected for being spiritually sound
Mirroring his heavenly Father who will never let you down.

Independence Day

July 4th, 1776 is a special birthday that we celebrate each year
The birth of our nation that deserves jubilation and cheer.
The Declaration of Independence paved the way for the American dream.
It affirms that all people are created equal and held with esteem.
Our founding fathers took many risks to provide these gifts
Of freedom, the pursuit of happiness and justice for all.
With a promise to not settle for less, they answered the call.
Independence Day is a day to honor our founders and sacrifices made
With hope that the values of integrity and truth would never fade.
They established a new nation to offer these inalienable rights.
To make certain God always will keep us in His sight.
Pray that our hearts will turn toward God
To ensure that He continues to pour out His blessing
Protecting our right to live free and avoid regressing.
The Pledge of Allegiance should remain unchanged
And The Bill of Rights and our Constitution not rearranged.
We must accept our differences and be thankful we live in the USA.
Victory will come for those who walk in faith and continue to pray
With confidence that our country as founded will never be led astray.

Presents or Presence

Should Christmas be all about the presents
You give and receive often with acquiescence?
Or is it about the lights that decorate the tree
That at Christmas time you love to see?

Could it be the presence you feel
Deep inside your heart that is real
When God comes into your heart
Finds a home and becomes a part?

The eyes that see the light
Shining in the dark of night
Will receive the lasting treasure
Not always as easy to measure.

So next year when you don't remember the presents
You'll still feel His holy and ever-loving presence.

Flower of the Holy Night

Often called the Flower of the Holy Night—
The poinsettia is a familiar Christmas sight
Symbolizing community spirit and good will.
Its vibrancy causes hearts to be still
While peace and tranquility fill the air
As a reminder to be thankful for God's loving care.
Poinsettias are red, white or pink in color
Representing the season to rediscover
The true meaning of our Christmas joy
To celebrate the birthday of a miracle baby boy.
When admiring the Christmas poinsettia,
Notice that the shape of the leaves resembles a star
Similar to the star of Bethlehem that shone from afar
Guiding the wisemen as they travelled searching to find
Hope that the Messiah can change a world that is unkind.
The red-colored leaves represent the blood
That washed away our sins like a cleansing flood.
The white leaves represent the baby's purity
Along with the assurance of redemption and security.
The Flower of the Holy Night—
December's birth flower
Brings forth a subtle mystique of power
Through its reflective spirit of Christmas joy
To welcome Jesus, the newborn baby boy.

Love Letters

CHAPTER 12

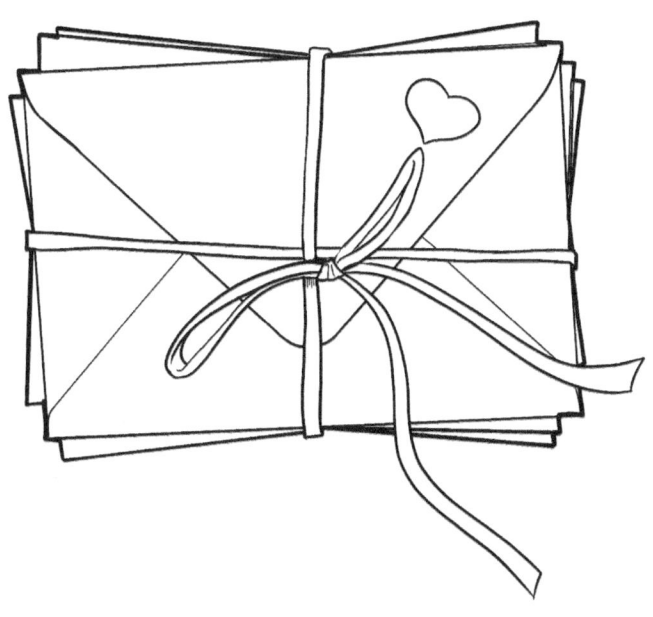

A Love Letter From My Heart

A love letter written from my heart
Contains a renewal of vows at the start
Like a romance movie montage
And a picture-perfect collage.
It reaches deep into my soul
Revealing things I've never told.
A heart does not forget
Even when it has paid the debt.
It looks forward to a bright new day
When tears have been washed away.
Each morning with you I am renewed
Without you I feel lost and confused.
I have faith when I cannot see
That's the way love should be.

When Loneliness Lingers

Elvis Presley often sang about the Heartbreak Hotel at the end of Lonely Street
Hoping his complex feeling of loneliness would start to retreat.
Today loneliness is an epidemic and a major wellness concern
Where disappointment seems to meet you at every turn.
Solitude in small doses is good for the soul
But as a constant state it will take its toll.
Music can be a refuge as you lose yourself in the notes
Turning your back on all that loneliness promotes.
Although many songs emphasize how lonely people feel
By changing a few words they will have a more positive appeal.
The Beatles sang the words, "Ah, look at all the lonely people."
Instead, they could have visualized people acting happy and gleeful.
Celine Dion crooned, "Don't wanna be all by myself anymore."
Why wasn't she searching for all the joy that was in store?
Taylor Swift sang, "We're happy, free, confused, and lonely at the same time."
But with hope why not say there is no mountain that we can't climb?
Akon chanted, "Lonely, I'm so lonely, I have nobody to call my own."
This refrain reflects today's sentiment of feeling all alone.
Instead of staying isolated, search for ways to be consoled
So loneliness no longer lingers and can be controlled.
Personal transformations require human effort
So that a happier end result becomes apparent.
If a weed patch can turn into a garden
Lingering loneliness can subside to erase or pardon
The bitterness, depression, withdrawal and isolation
And become the motivation to improve your situation.
When God is by your side, loneliness often becomes a path
To a more fulfilling life without feelings of apathy and wrath.

A Season of Uncertainty

When your future seems blurry
And your mind is in a flurry
You hold back the tears
Because life is so dear.
You take a deep breath
To comprehend the depth
Of what lies ahead for you
As love continues to shine through.
Inside you find it hard
To accept this dreaded card
That life has just dealt
Fearing your heart might melt.
Life is not the same as it used to be
Things have changed a massive degree——
Loving is deeper than you thought possible
And compassion and benevolence is unstoppable.
When someone close to you is treading water
You are the life raft and strongest supporter
So when life throws out curve balls
You have the strength to stop or stall
The uncertainty of another day
Even when launched in each and every way.
Because of your strong faith and trust
God allows you time to readjust
As you are led through the storm
Seeing He has the power to transform
A season of uncertainty
Into a healing path to recovery.

A Friend Like You

Helen Keller once said
"I would rather walk with a friend in the dark
Than alone in the light."
A true friend sympathizes with your current plight
Composes a beautiful song from their heart
Then sings it softly so you don't fall apart.
Sometimes you meet someone who just clicks
Like a fine-tuned clock that consistently ticks.
You never have to pretend to be anyone or anything
They know the burden you have been carrying.
Great friendship is irreplaceable;
A friend's value is unmistakable.
They inspire you to be a better person
Without any unnecessary or forced coercion.
This is why they are your best friend
A person on which you can always depend.
They are all the therapy you need
Because they listen and take heed
Call you to check if you're okay
Bake Irish brownies to bring your way.
A friend like that makes life worthwhile
Especially on a day you see their radiant smile.
That's a day you will cry less and laugh harder
Unlocking your heart from its shield of armor.

Never Again

How many times do you say never
And you think you are being so clever
Until temptation breaks you down
Making it harder each time to rebound.
Then unexpectedly all your doubts disappear
And a new horizon of atonement appears
With a ray of light shining down upon you
Erasing fears; extending mercies that are new.
No longer are you chasing after false hope
You have come to the end of your rope.
Suddenly strength overtakes weakness
As God spawns your significant uniqueness.
Prayers have been answered
Reconciliation is transferred
You have found your fortress
Never again to be support-less.
You are renewed with every breath you take
Promises made are now promises kept.
You've seen the truth and a new way
No more lies, only blessings...
Never again to be led astray.

Reflections

CHAPTER 13

Reflections on a Lake

In the afternoon as the sun goes down
Serene and quiet with only a few birds around
Reflections on a lake begin to appear
Faint images of the landscape become clear.
The still waters of a lake reflect the beauty around it
A pattern of land and water that God has knit
So they seem as one, no beginning or end
Trees are reflected and colors blend.
Green, red and yellow hues can be observed
A second little world where hope is reaffirmed.
Homes frame the lake as birds fly overhead
Sounds of nature reverberate while not a word is said.
Reflections are peacefully still and endlessly inspiring
A landscape's most expressive feature is forever beguiling.
When ripples form on the surface of a lake
Its depth cannot be seen because it becomes opaque.
The same is true when your mind is troubled and not at rest
The harmony within your heart is never felt or expressed.

Motivation and Empowerment

Sometimes you feel like you are all alone
Powerless to act when on your own—
Without motivation to muster up the energy
To rise above the haze of mental lethargy.
Pray for strength to lift yourself out of the cloud
Into the sunlight where God's love is allowed.
Tap into a source of power to ignite your way
Become empowered because it's a new day
To sing a song of hope written for all to sing
Or dance a new dance for the joy it brings.
Brush away the malaise that has held you down
Face the sun and let your feet touch the ground.
Be thankful that you can share a new testimony
Not expecting accolades, an award, or a ceremony.
Every day is a gift with an opportunity for you to share
Love, compassion, positive thoughts and a daily prayer.

Lost in the Hazy Sun

What happened to all the fun
Did it get lost in the hazy sun?
Each day was filled with smiles
And you could walk for miles
Laughing and enjoying the conversation
Without obstacles to clear communication.
Trips and vacations have been put on hold
Along with the excitement of being bold.
Singing happy birthday has lost its appeal
Life has changed and now seems surreal.
You can choose to have a pity party
Or take a cue from Vince Lombardi
Who made history by winning super-bowls
Against the odds with faith and a worthy goal.
Don't let the situation get the best of you
Turn it over to God to help you pull through——
No longer blind-sighted by the hazy sun
As the sky clears showing that healing has begun.

A Light Against Darkness

Often someone will catch you off guard
Initiating a feeling of vulnerability you cannot disregard.
Try to let go of any negative reaction
Even if it creates a sense of dissatisfaction.
You may think that what they say is wrong
Disagree with a viewpoint that seems too strong.
Unverbalized thoughts need to stay that way
Save them for another time but not today.
Think it over before saying something you regret
If you just walk away no one will get upset.
It's not worth creating an enemy or losing a friend
Be the person others will count on and can depend.
Never be one to condemn, criticize, or complain
Leaving an uncomfortable aura to remain.
Instead ask God to be their light against darkness
He alone can bring peace to smooth out harshness.

Oh What a Beautiful Morning

Four golfers, two golf carts, and four Sandhill cranes
All appeared one morning as far as I could ascertain
When looking across the lake to the golf course tee
Of Sweetgum executive course for hole number three.

It was a recipe for a good binocular sighting
Making this sunny morning all the more inviting.
These surroundings came alive as I began to awake
Sensing a rhythm of reflection like shadows on a lake.

If you take time each day to observe and ponder
Allowing yourself to be still so your mind can't wander
You'll discover that it is always a beautiful morning
When your attitude reflects a fresh new dawning.

As you observe simple things like the fluttering of birds
You will be pleasantly surprised and lost for words.
It's possible to catch the sun rising if the sky is clear
Creating a majestic sight to suddenly appear.

Billowing waves of serenity will fill your mind
To overcome yesterday's fears that are left behind
So you can experience God's glorious new day in total focus
Establishing harmony, synergy and a natural symbiosis.

The Power of Keeping a Promise

A commitment to follow through is essential
It is a promise made that can be consequential.
If your word can't be trusted it affects other people
Creating misunderstanding and personal upheaval.
A half-hearted commitment won't make the grade
And a successful conclusion may never be made.
Perseverance takes energy but is worth it in the end
Halfheartedness and lack of priority is hard to defend.
If a promise is not kept then a bond is broken
By excuses made and secrets not spoken.
Learn from mistakes and become a truth seeker
Realizing that God is the ultimate promise keeper.

The Inevitable Fate of Earrings

CHAPTER 14

The Inevitable Fate of Earrings

When rushing around the house trying to be on time
Thinking I'm retired, being late is not a crime.
Doesn't it seem like everyone always gets there way ahead?
Sometimes you oversleep and decide to stay longer in bed.

You worry that people may stop and stare
If you don't do something with your hair.
What do you think holds you up the most
Is it applying makeup to avoid looking like a ghost?

Or is it deciding what to wear
When your favorite pair of leggings has a tear?
Then there are your teeth that you have to brush
Adding to the feeling that you have to rush.

Plus you need to start using that new water pick
Wow, if only you could still call in sick!
Often you eat your breakfast in the car
Gobble it down because it's not too far.

If someone asks why are you always late
Blame it on your earrings, let it be their fate.
It takes forever to put four earrings onto your ears
Especially when frustrated and close to tears.

Why not take a friend's advice not to wear earrings anymore
So when all else fails, just throw them all out the door?
Do you wonder why you ever decided to pierce a second hole
One in each ear is plenty, how did you get so out of control?

Retirement is supposed to be a time to relax
Not feel like you are always running away from an ax.
You should be slowing down, going along with the flow
Not packing your schedule so you're constantly on the go.

Brooms, Handles, and New Puppies

Do you sweep things under the rug
To keep a secret with just a shrug
Or hide something you don't want anyone to know
Hoping that with time it will never show?
The idiom is based on a story of a lazy housekeeper or maid
Who tried to take shortcuts and still get paid.

Brooms are used to keep your house neat
Not for sweeping someone off their feet
Hoping they will fall in love with you on the spot
Get to know you better and give you a shot.
This metaphor suggests knocking a person over or down
To make a good impression in hopes of sticking around.

Sometimes you need to get a handle on your emotions
Before you fly off the handle causing a commotion
Meaning you tend to get extremely irritable and angry
Not able to handle simple situations
So friends think you must always be "hangry.

Now you can't seem to handle your new little puppy
Thinking instead you should have gotten a guppy.
Once you get a grip, the puppy will be easier to handle
Before you get out the broom and cause a big scandal.
Puppy love will grow as you settle into a routine
The broom can then be used for circumstances unforeseen.

Stitches

You had me in stitches
When you needed stitches for your britches.
Laughing out loud or sewing and mending
Whatever meaning you are apprehending.

Have you heard the idiom: a stitch in time saves nine?
Another way of saying don't put it off for a later time
It's better to deal with a problem right away
Than to procrastinate and have a price to pay.

I have seven stitches in my head
Because I fell out of bed.
Sutures or stitches sometimes follow surgery
Whether planned or due to an emergency.

A stitch can denote a stabbing puncture or pain
Not easy to describe or try to explain.
A stitch is also a person who is very funny
Makes your day seem bright and sunny.

Shawn Mendes recorded Stitches, now a popular song
And a line dance was choreographed to go along.
Lilo and Stitch are characters in a Disney movie
Likable but mischievous; nothing ever goes smoothly.

Stitches is also a 2012 comedy horror film
About a clown's revenge that becomes quite grim.
What ever happened to Stitches, the rapper, who sang Brick in Yo Face?
I heard, due to his stitches tattoo, he was teleported into hyperspace.

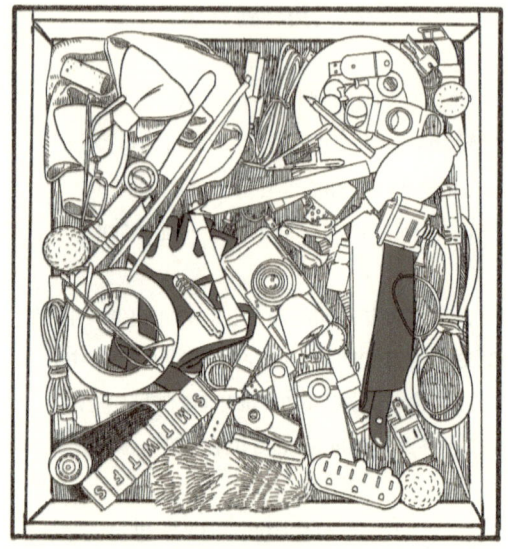

The Junk Drawer

Can't find a paper clip or rubber band
Didn't you drop one yesterday, where did it land?
Why not check the junk drawer?
You'll find that and lots more
Including all types of unrelated and unorganized objects
Such as screwdrivers, pliers, tape measures, and old specs
Scissors, glue, tape, birthday candles, pencils and pens
Thumbtacks, binder clips, push pins, and a magnifying lens.

Every couple of years you need to clean out the junk drawer
Before it gets unruly, over stuffed and quite an eyesore
Then miraculously it repopulates and fills up again.
Why do we have junk drawers, it's hard to comprehend?
It is a great place to hide an odd number of corn-on-the-cob holders
A rubber band ball, picture hangers, pins and a couple of coasters.
You might also find hot pads, buttons, twist ties, and solo cup lids
Along with birthday cards and other items left from the kids.
Surely you need to keep all these items like an odd pair of socks
Plus out-of-date reminders and toothpicks that fell out of the box.
Maybe you'll find key rings, old keys or a bill you never paid
And a whole host of other junk that you meant to throw away.
Sometimes you may feel that your mind is similar to a junk drawer
You know it's time to get rid of bad habits you tend to ignore
Throwing out feelings of weakness, anxiety and things you can't control
Including all those should-haves, would-ofs and unattainable goals.
Clear out the excuses and regrets that stop you from moving forward
Leaving room for God's love and blessings as your greatest reward.

Walk Away the Frowns

Have you ever met a Surly Shirley
Always acting like she is in a hurry
Usually with a frown on her face
Even when walking at a steady pace?
One afternoon when 3 friends were walking on a narrow path
They passed a Surly Shirley emanating a look of wrath.
Did we cause her to move a little off to the side
Slightly interrupting her steady stride?
We were courteous so she didn't have to go around
But thinking she needs a class called "Walk Away the Frowns"
To learn that a smile is often better than riches and wealth
Erasing anguish and despair to help improve overall health.
A frown is an expression of displeasure and gloom
Whereas a person with a smile can light up a room
Lifting the mood and alleviating stress
Wiping away a frown with total success.

Dancing on the Edges of Your Heart

CHAPTER 15

Dancing on the Edges of Your Heart

When someone dances on the edges of your heart
Not intentionally wanting to tear it apart
You begin to feel that things have been rearranged
And the light has dimmed and its intensity changed.
When emotions find a home but have no place to hide
They will need to be released instead of being set aside.
When you experience the familiar pain of heartbreak
And you don't understand or know what's at stake
You may have to travel through some darkness
Before seeing the light of hope and future happiness.
When someone dances on the edges of your soul
Be sure they step lightly without losing control
So they don't make scars that are slow to mend
Leaving unresolved grief and regret that may transcend.

It All Comes Down to Faith

In life you often go through a restless streak
When life is dark and seems so bleak
And you're waiting for the storm to pass
Bringing a better and brighter forecast.
During this time it all comes down to faith
Along with unshakable trust in every case.
Faith is evidence of things you cannot see
Believing that God is in control is the key.
In this world everything is not perfect
Bad things happen that you can't neglect.
Your faith is tested when you face a challenge
Or when your normal life is out of balance.
Doubt will weaken your strength and resolve
As God answers prayers fear begins to dissolve.

Turning a Blind Eye and the Three Wise Monkeys

Have you met "see no evil," hear no evil," and "speak no evil"
The 3 wise monkeys who often cause an upheaval?
A 4th monkey "do no evil" sometimes is part of the famous quote.
There are various meanings to what the proverb denotes—
Looking the other way, feigning ignorance, or turning a blind eye
Sticking your head in the sand or gazing up at the sky.
The image of the 3 monkeys symbolizes a lack of moral responsibility

On the part of people who refuse to acknowledge impropriety.
Today many people turn a blind eye to things illegal or bad
Pretend not to notice or refuse to acknowledge, which is sad.
Do you care enough to help those oppressed or in need?
You are never too young or old to help others succeed.
What if God turned a blind eye on you, the U.S., the world
Letting an evil force take over as hatred is unfurled?
Therefore, do not turn your back but show you care
Remaining strong, focused, and aware.
So open your eyes and take a stand
You have a sympathetic heart that wants to lend a hand
With a powerful mind to exert a positive influence
As the earth and heavens meet establishing a continuance.

Red-Zone Woes

You're in the red zone and you can't get out
So close to crossing the goal line wanting to shout.
Caught in this trap is like being stuck in gridiron traffic
Wishing you could relocate to a new demographic.
Wild emotions are galloping all over the place
This definitely is not how you started this race.
When marooned in the red zone
Stranded inside the unknown
It's time to focus on a new strategy
That might include a recharge of your battery.
Red-zone inertia is the penalty when unable to move
Painful and destructive until you get into the groove
Of a new path far from the one you now travel
To avoid getting tackled and begin to unravel.
After you have had enough, ask God for a reprieve
He will restore, support, and help you to achieve
A firm foundation outside of the proverbial red zone
Assured you don't have to face these woes all alone.

All the Moving Parts

A life is made up of many moving parts
All of which are connected to the heart
From the time you wake up in the morning
Until night when dreams turn into warnings.
At the time you were conceived and born
Life was fragile and each day was a new dawn
Body, mind, and spirit became conjoined
Into a world where love is transformed.
As we plot our path through all the moving parts
Weaving a web of mental and physical marks
We are affected by positive and negative forces
From many diverse and sundry sources.
There will be joyful births and painful deaths
Along with heartaches; simple and complex
When what is normal seems jaded
Our memories may become faded.
We adapt to transitions and fresh starts
Among the new and old moving parts
Adjusting and operating among changes
As the stages of life are rearranging.
God will be there as the engineer
Guiding us away from danger and fear
He is the potter who spins the wheel
As we love, respond, reach and feel.

Icing on the Cake

CHAPTER 16

Icing on the Cake

Icing or frosting on a cake is yummy and delicious
But not considered very nutritious.
Most people love its glorious sweet taste
Decorating a cake when artistically placed
For a birthday party, holiday or other special occasion
When friends and family get together at a specific location.
It can intensify the moment by creating a certain theme
Adding excitement to the celebration enhancing the dream.
Especially for a wedding, a decadent cake can make the day
Spectacularly designed in an exceptional way.
"Icing on the cake" is also an idiom or saying
You probably have heard what it is conveying.
There are two meanings that happen to be opposite
Making a good situation better is the most predominate.
Changing a bad situation into something worse
Hopefully is not one that is par for the course.
What is your example of experiencing "icing on the cake"
Eating your favorite meal that you didn't have to make?
Is it that special someone who is the center of your life
And you're enjoying a nice evening without any strife?
On the other hand it could be a difficult day
When nothing seems to be going your way.
A bad day is made worse by some unexpected news
You got hurt, can't dance, and have the pity-party blues.

The Familiarity Trap

Being in love is more than a state of mind
Especially if you believe your love is one of a kind.
Is happiness also just a state of mind
Excluding unplanned events that can be unkind?
Happiness settles in when your heart feels joy
Along with a feeling of peace it tries to employ.
We tend to label things and experiences
That are repeated often with subtle variances.
For instance, when you see someone cry
You usually think that sadness applies
But do you ever consider an alternative explanation
That the person crying could be chopping an onion
Or maybe just acting or laughing so hard
That tears begin flowing catching you off guard?
Perhaps you are stuck in the familiarity trap
When reality and illusion are causing a gap.
Autopilot sets in so you are too busy to think
Going through the motions trying not to sink.
You could be automatically heading in the wrong direction
Unaware of decisions made and resultant implications.
Welcome to another hook of the familiarity trap
When you search high and low not to find the right app
Until opportunities vanish and your view becomes narrow.
The answer is to unplug, unwind and focus on what's important
Talk to God; He is invariably your most trustworthy informant.

Same Heartache, Different Day

Same heartache, different day
Same game, different play
Same dance, different phrasing
Same sunset, differently amazing
Same storm, different threat
Same situation, different way to forget
Same silhouette, different year
Same person, different fear
Same relationship, different time
Same trouble, different wine
Same children, different directive
Same friends, different perspective
Same age, different dimension
Same year, different direction
Same situation, different feeling
Same life, different way of dealing
Same prayer, different answers
Same music, different dancers
Same God, never changing
Same life, always rearranging.

The Unguarded Heart

The unguarded heart is vulnerable to attack
From enemies that are hard to track.
They come from within and without
So stay diligent and do not doubt
How they may affect your fragile heart.
It is easy to monitor daily behavior and actions
But protecting the heart is not a normal reaction.
A heart is so intricate and complicated
Its mysterious conduct is not easily regulated.
Words we speak originate in the heart—
The control center for all other parts
Stabilizing and directing how we live and relate.
Often our expressions tend to exaggerate
Our secret sensitivities and insensitivities
As they intersect with our routine activities.
Guardrails are needed to keep us on the right path
Like a dreamcatcher sifting out dreams of wrath
Filtering out tainted illusions and deceptive lies
That sound good but are pitfalls in disguise.
For the most part we can control what comes about
By remaining diligent to protect an unguarded heart
So we can sleep peacefully without stress.
In Proverbs, King Solomon says it best:
"Above all else, guard your heart,
for it is the wellspring of life."

Cultivating a Pure and Generous Heart

To avoid interference you often put on your headset
Just as a heart avoids adversity with an uncluttered mindset
That eventually evolves into a generous and giving heart
With love for others forming the major part.
A pure heart directs and guides thoughts and actions
Away from all the world's many distractions.
In most cases, a generous heart will put others first
So that emotions do not blend together and are blurred.
It is easy to focus on trivial things that don't matter
Causing your priorities to shift and shatter.
Generosity and sacrifice seem to be counter to a culture
That pecks away at your values like a ravenous vulture.
The problem comes when your possessions take control
And you are unable to set positive and worthy goals.
Look for ways to cultivate a pure and generous heart
By taking the first step to make God the central part
Of every waking moment so His presence begins to shine through
In many different ways by all you say and do.

The Renewal of Your Mind

Don't expect miracles to happen for you
If you're trying to bite off more than you can chew.
Sift through the chaos in your mind
Leaving the negative thoughts behind
So your mind is not a sidewalk for evil to enter.
You need a spiritual anchor like God as the center,
Soil that is rich and fertile for goodness to grow
And what remains in your heart is what will show.
The same sun that melts ice also hardens clay
If you show gratefulness, mercy will strengthen the way.
Positive thoughts won't stay if they are not assisted
Negative thoughts won't leave when they are not resisted.
Your mind needs a border to keep obstructive influences out
Only then can an efficacious ebb and flow settle throughout.
Take a daily inventory of words spoken and personal interactions
So that a renewal of your mind will be a receptive transaction.
According to 2 Corinthians 4:16, "our outer self is wasting away
As our inner self is being renewed day by day."

Just Because It's Raining

CHAPTER 17

Just Because It's Raining

In your hurting, sorrow and desperation
You pray for healing and a clear explanation
Hoping that your circumstances will change
Releasing a breakthrough to help rearrange.
Just because it's raining now
The sun will shine when the weather allows.
How much heartache can one heart hold
Can it stretch so much that it's no longer bold?
If you feel helpless and at the end of your rope
Dig deep and you'll see there's always hope.
No two situations are the same
Stay strong, don't transfer the blame
Take responsibility so a solution comes to mind
If you listen there is an answer that you'll find.
God will show you how to conquer these impediments
To rise above the streams of harmonic sentiments.

Make Every Day Count

Don't waste time, make the most of it
Because life throws curve balls as it sees fit.
We are faced with challenges every day
We get hurt, grieve and must look for a better way.
Be creative to make each day meaningful and worthwhile
We only have so much time on this earth so why not smile.
If each day includes activities and achievements that count
Then mountains wouldn't seem so hard to surmount.
We have our own ideas of what matters in life
But sometimes you have to listen to sound advice.
There are simple things to do to have a purposeful day
Express heartfelt gratitude and give thanks without delay.
Get most of your tasks done early so you have more time
To do the things that keep your purpose in mind.
God will guide you toward worthy goals and trends
Allowing time with loved ones and other friends.
Do something that helps to improve your health
You'll find it matters more than gaining wealth.
Have a good laugh everyday to keep your mood light
Worries, fears and doubts soon will start to take flight.
Get out of your comfort zone by doing something new
There are so many bucket-list items you have yet to pursue.
Remove distractions that get in the way
Try setting a time to talk to God every day
A habit to calm the turbulent waters of your heart
Metamorphosing into an untrodden new start.

Purple Skies

The sky becomes purple with the approaching dawn
As the combination of pink and dark hues begins to spawn.
After a hurricane arrives leaving rain and a low cloud cover
A dark purple sky often appears when the storm no longer hovers.

Other factors come into play that can jumble the light
When pollen, dust and pollution move into sight.
The color purple is somewhat of a mystery
Whether part of the sky or someone's color history.

When the sky is purple it can mean someone will go on a journey
Of self-discovery leading to a spiritual awakening each morning?
Always pay attention to your dreams and intuitions
Listening intently for messages about infinite possibilities.

Recently all I see are purple overcast skies
And I don't understand how or why.
Darkness surrounds me on most days
Like there is an overhanging ominous haze.

If pink clouds are superimposed on a sky that is dark blue
Will hope be found within the pink clouds as a clue
Indicating that situations in my life will cease to be so dire
As God's healing rays shine through illuminating like a fire.

Dreaming of Blue Skies

Seems easy — just close your eyes
Drift away dreaming of blue skies
Sunshine, roses and easier days
Showing our love in so many ways.

Now I toss and turn still awake
Wishing this is all a big mistake
Afraid of being on my own.
Longing for days back in the zone
Sharing our thoughts and desires
Doing everything that love requires.

Longing to travel together and walk for miles
Now I am happy just to see your smiles.
Will it ever be the same?
I feel too old to play this game
Of overcoming another loss
Not knowing what toll it will cost.

I pray for a miracle to take place
Knowing God controls life's pace
So I can fall asleep without a worry
Ready to begin a new chapter to our story.

The Lion

CHAPTER 18

The Lion Inside

There is a lion inside of me
That no one else can see
Providing powerful spiritual wealth
As its shadow passes by with stealth.
It provides blessings to be redeemed
And is worthy of respect and esteem.
It lives within my heart and mind
Gives me strength but tells me to be kind.
The lion inside tackles fear and makes it cease
So it is never allowed to further increase.
It bestows peace furnishing solace to my soul
So stress and anxiety no longer take control.
Its voice tells me that I still have a song to sing
Poems to write, bells to ring
And a new dance to dance
Giving me courage to take a chance.
So when the lion inside roars
Its power and potential soars
Then healing is restored.

Awaken

Be attuned and ready to change
Your life's itinerary is not so hard to rearrange.
When you are open to learning new things
You become more excited for what each day brings.

Have you ever felt a tug to take a different route
Even if you're not sure where it leads or what it's about?
You may feel compelled to speak to a stranger
Or reach out to a troubled friend
But you are too busy
Not wanting to change direction or try to bend.

You ignored the feeling, not wanting to give advice
Too consumed by what is going on in your own life.
Or conversely, go overboard to support someone else
Only to feel you are losing control of yourself.

Life should be a balance of giving and taking
Empathy is a must not to be forsaken.
Growing old has some ups but many downs
Where compassion is felt like a soft mist that surrounds.

Awaken to the sound of each breath
Refreshing your soul with its depth.
Pray with boldness out of expectation
As God moves beyond all human imagination.

Waves of Heartbreak

Standing in the middle of a stormy sea
As waves are crashing down on me
Trying not to slip or fall down
To be tossed about and all around
Washed far away and forgotten
Because without him I will be forsaken.

In life we have ups and downs
And smiles become hidden by the frowns
But when the downs decide to take over
Heartbreak increases with each exposure
Washing away dreams a little more each day
Trying not to lose the will to pray.

I've exhausted most of my patience
Now my prayers seem less efficacious.
Every day the tears build up a little more
Eventually the dam will break with a mighty roar.
Like a beaver I try to build up hope
Developing more resistance to stay afloat.

Keeping busy helps control the sadness
When will I smile again with sheer gladness
Feel tenderness like a soft breeze on my face
Instead of having to gather up a bit of grace.

When sadness fills my heart
I try hard not to fall apart
I do know God is in control
Staying by my side to console.

Crying in the Night

Was it a dream…
Or did I hear you crying
As I couldn't help sighing
In the silence of the night
Too afraid to cry in the light.

Was it a dream…
Either way my heart was broken
As no words were being spoken
Just the sorrow that broke free
Touching deep inside of me.

Was it a dream…
Filling me with an unwanted fear
That I heard the sound of a tear
As the mist of darkness seemed to linger
Waiting for the light of day to softly glimmer.

Was it a dream…
Or did God appear to bring healing
With an answer He is revealing
So crying heard in the night
Will bring hope with the morning light.

Living on a Seesaw

CHAPTER 19

Living on a Seesaw

Highs and lows
Is how life goes
Hoping each new day
Brings a brighter promise
Before turning into a doubting Thomas.

Hope seems to disappear
Praying it will reappear.
Sanity is nowhere to be found
Even when there is not a sound.

Each day brings something new
Erasing smiles to just a few.
When the seesaw goes up,
It becomes easier to cope.
But as it goes down,
It's more difficult to stay afloat.

Coming home trying not to shout
Is it selfish to sit and pout?
Trying to maintain a stable level
While having to chase away the devil.

Change is part of every day
Looking for a better way
Waiting for a positive call
When living on a seesaw.

The Tipping Point

Reaching the tipping point when young or old
Could whirl you into a panic mode
And separate you from a sense of reality
Eventually giving you a lack of vitality.

A sudden shock that relays a bad situation
Catapults you into the fear of isolation.
Don't allow yourself to jump to hasty conclusions
It only will lead to unnecessary mental confusion.

A tipping point tells you that change is inevitable
Although it doesn't always have to be irrevocable.
Suddenly your future travels into the twilight zone
Acting like a zombie flailing around in the unknown.

Get a grip, reach out to someone who will console
A friend who can relate and play a healing role.
Your tipping point can hit before you have time to review
Hold on tight to God knowing He understands you.
In His timeline He will answer all your prayers
With His infinite wisdom because He truly cares.

Keep the Candle Burning

Keep the candle burning
With the light of love shining
Paving the way through impending darkness
With its graceful glow of brilliance.

As the candle burns with a healing vibe
Hearts, minds and souls come alive
Never allowing its fluorescence to dim
Perfectly adding to a heart's radiant trim.

For now, our recent trials and trends
Need God's light to heal and mend.
So if heartaches evaporate into the sky
We can stop having to ask why.

As the clouds hold back the rain
Easing harm to nature's grain
Then all the pain and raw emotions
Will fade like the tide that controls the oceans.

Although the world seems filled with madness
Causing a blanket of fear and sadness
Keep the candle burning with the hope
That God controls its breadth and scope.

The Guilt Trip

A guilt trip is not a trip you want to take
It is a path that only an unsettled mind will make.
Worry is its tour guide that hinders daily progress
Not adding a single second of time only extra stress.

Don't lose sleep over what may or may not come
It is a waste of time that leaves you feeling glum.
Guilt is a powerful motivator of human behavior
Inflicted as a menacing device not in your favor.

Don't give in and let someone control your emotions
Guilt-tripping conduct can cause personal erosion
Employing the silent treatment as a major elusive tool
That causes you to feel isolated and an antagonistic fool.

If someone makes you feel bad about something you have done
Or didn't do, so you do them a favor knowing they have won.
You have been led astray traveling on an unnecessary guilt trip
Learn from it so not to be tricked and forced to slip.

Don't allow anyone to make you feel guilty
Take control, don't yield thinking that you are faulty.
You should not feel responsible or compelled to change
Do what you know is right and let God take the reins.

The Horror Show

Where are the flowers that no longer grow
When you're starring in a horror show?
Goblins and ghosts will gather near
Creating waves of doubt and fear.

Where is the passion and the kiss
Gone along with the happy days of bliss?
Each day adds more weight to carry
In an atmosphere that's way too scary.

Where are the sunlight serenades
Are they disguised as a game of charades?
Day by day the light gets dimmer
As the threat of darkness simmers.

Where are the soft summer breezes
Now the cold wind blows then freezes
Swept away with the love that once filled the air
But I find comfort knowing You hear my prayer.

Waiting for the New Dawn

CHAPTER 20

Waiting for the New Dawn

After several seasons in the wilderness
While overcoming unrelenting fearfulness
I learned that nothing is wasted with God
Everything experienced is not a façade.
The journey included many dead-end roads
Without any directions or secret codes
But a deeper love and closeness to others not felt before
Came like soft rays of light shining through an open door.
A deeper sense of God's presence floated everywhere
Making it easier to breathe because of calmness in the air.
All this led to a new array of emotions
Easing the flux of frantic commotion
Culminating into a tranquil sense of peace
While waiting for the new dawn's release.

No Apology Necessary

Don't apologize because your life reflects God's presence
Your life has a purpose to fulfill of obvious quintessence.
Only apologize when you are truly wrong
It is the only way to show that you are strong.
Don't apologize for a day when you feel happy
On most days you have more than you can carry.
Don't apologize if you are not sincere
Make the words you speak ring crystal clear.
Don't apologize for feeling blessed
Be happy you have someone to caress.

Try not to long for what you don't have or can't see
Even if everything is not how you hoped it would be.
Life is too short to always say you're sorry
The answer is to always give God the glory.
Be happy for other people and don't keep score
Isn't that what friends are for?
Does love require that you always apologize
Or are your actions and persona enough to justify?
When you realize that for everything there is a season
No apology is necessary without a meritable reason.

Love's Symphony

What if every song you sing is a symphony
That results in a sense of wonder or epiphany?
The words have the aura of divine intervention
That's deserving of praise and special attention.
It is a symphony of love and life's perfect melody
Coming deeper from within as a remedy
To soothe and comfort the pain
Knowing life as it was will not be the same.

What if every dance you dance gives a sensation
Of pure love and a feeling of elation
As your dance generates awe and wonder
Like lightning and rolling thunder?
But this dance becomes just an illumination
Of a broken heart's manifestation
Too harrowing to dance again with the same beat
As its rhythm has shifted with no way to repeat.

A Heart's Disguise

I wish I knew how long I will be crying over you
Not knowing how much more I can go through.
There's always a new way a heart can ache
Not sure if anyone hears it when it breaks.

Can you see it in my eyes?
I know it is very hard to disguise.
Maybe it is best to let it show
Then it will give others a chance to know.

It's been a long time waiting for love to sing its serenade
When we'd smile, laugh and dance as the moonlight fades
Holding each other tight never wanting to let go.
What happens when the curtain closes on the show?

Will someone say the words that bring healing
While suffering with the pain I am feeling
You have touched my eyes then my heart
Now how do I face the hardest part?

The only way I know is to lean on God as my guide
He is always here constantly by my side
Listening because He knows and understands.
So now I have to let go…
Allowing God to take me by the hand.

When a Week Seems Like a Month

One moment in time can change your life
Shifting its direction to an unfamiliar design.
You always feared this could happen to you
But now this bad dream has really come true.

A week seems like a month
When each day has struggles to confront.
To sleep through the night is a gift
When your state of mind has made this shift.

To hold back tears then wonder why
They are stuck in your head or up in the sky
Afraid the dam will break causing a flood
Hitting the ground with a thunderous thud.

Emotions are flying north, south, east and west
A week is like a lifetime passing slowly at best.
Being alone is not what you're used to
I guess it's just a new phase you have to go through.

The Wonderful Wizard

PART 2

The Wonderful Wizard

Every animal deserves a chance
You will find this out at first glance.
When you meet the Wizard for the first time
Your curiosity will peak and begin to realign
With stories that will touch your heart
You may even shed a tear as a part

Of seeing the Wizard's incredible ability to create prostheses
For animals helping them to walk once more
Providing hope and solving problems you have not seen before.
The best part is watching the animals
Become restored to health right before your eyes.
For example, there is a lovable dog named Toto.
His legs were badly damaged in a farm accident
But his transformation is more than miraculous
At the work of the Wizard's skillful hands.
If you focus on Toto's new prosthetic legs you'll understand
How people can quickly become huge fans
As more animals like Toto learn to walk again without fear and pain
And you discover all that can be gained
By giving hope to the hopeless.
This is the beautiful theme intertwined throughout
That you'll discover without a doubt.
As each heartwarming real-life story is unfurled
The Wonderful Wizard brings sunshine to your world.

Inspiration is a Two-Way Street

Do owners inspire their pets
So that pets are always in their debt
Providing shelter, food and care
And things that make pets more aware?

Or is it the other way around?
Animals give back more with love that abounds
Inspiring owners by their courage and determination
With unconditional affection and devotion.

Dogs have evolved to become acutely attuned to humans.
They understand how to react without confusion
Keenly aware of their owners' behavior and emotions
Able to ask for what they want without a commotion.

Companionship and rapport go both ways
For a pet and an owner on any given day.
Inspiration is also a two-way street
Creating a bond that makes their lives complete.

In another story involving the Wizard
You met a farm dog named Lacie who answered the call
Of being an inspiration to us all.
Even though Lacie was paralyzed
Seeing her courage you soon realized
There existed a love for life, hope and gratitude.

So with the support of her family and a positive attitude
A special cart was designed by the the Wizard
To substitute for Lacie's damaged back legs and paws.
Lacie was finally able to run and play again
All coming together as a perfect inspirational blend.

Adapters

Adapters change to better fit their circumstances
In order to exist, survive and have better chances.
When we get married, move, or a new baby is born
We become adapters even when not forewarned.
In the environment adaptations are easy to see
Giraffes developed long necks for feeding in tall trees.
The human body sweats and dogs pant to cool the body.
A rabbit freezes sensing a predator is near but cannot see.
Americans made changes when faced with a pandemic
They adapted to try to control a nation-wide epidemic.

Animals often show humans how they adjust to survive
Whatever comes their way they adapt in order to stay alive.
The Wizard provides many of these examples.
Animals become adapters when strength and trust is ample.
A sanctuary in Vermont is a special farm
Where animals are rescued and protected from harm.
The story of Lois the cow will show
How she was given a second chance to walk and time to grow.
Even though her front legs were deformed
With the skill of the Wizard, hope was restored.
Lois adapted to the prosthetics that were specially designed
When faith, determination, and craftsmanship were aligned.
Because the Wizard arrived at this sanctuary farm
A miracle unfolded right before our eyes.
Lois learned to walk using her new legs like a charm.
Adapters survive when love and will power are in surplus.
All animals deserve a chance at life to fulfill their purpose.

Fighter Spirits

We are born with a fighter spirit.
Babies survive enormous odds just to be born.
Survival instincts help when facing life's storms.
As we grow older that fighter spirit becomes stronger
Overcoming our limitations in order to live longer.
The fight-or-flight instinct is triggered in a fearful situation
Creating a threat to our existence until we gather more information.
We should count each day we wake up as a miracle
Like climbing a mountain and reaching the pinnacle.

Frida is a dog who was helped by the Wizard.
She had a mountain to climb when faced with her flaws.
Her back legs were paralyzed and deformed creating a terrible situation.
The Wizard faced doubts that he could find the best solution.
He got to work and succeeded calling upon his own fighter spirit.
Frida was transformed to run again proving that a champion has no limit.

A dog named Zoey, from another Wizard story, was missing a leg.
Zoey's owner had also lost her leg and walked using a prosthetic instead.
The similarities of the two situations were too much alike to be ignored.
Zoey adapted to her prosthesis, crafted by the Wizard, so mobility was restored.
Is it possible that a dog senses her owner's fighter spirit and mission?
Then with the courage of warriors these unlikely miracles came to fruition.

All the Best Things

When all the best things come together
The satisfaction felt is difficult to measure.
The warmth of a newborn baby is the epitome of pureness
Hearts overflow with love and a sense of completeness.
Smaller life events occur if you're not afraid to take a chance
When you win a race, write a book, perform a new dance.
Or when a dog is rescued and adopted by a loving family
If not placed in their care, he could face a severe calamity.
Trigger is a dog like this who is in another Wizard story
His disability and limitations make you feel very sorry.
Trigger's pain and lack of mobility became a dire slippery slope
Until you discover how the family's guardianship provided hope.
A big step to a four-legged future for Trigger became probable
Because the Wizard's gifted hands once again made it all possible.
For Trigger's front legs he designed both a prosthesis and a brace
Allowing for a healthier life for Trigger to be put into place.

Striking a Chord in Your Heart

Pets can teach their owners many life lessons
With a pure and simple style void of human obsessions.
Pets seem to maintain a positive attitude through adversity
When given love and care they are happy in spite of disability.
Another story presents a challenge for the Wizard.
The needs of a small dog named Teo have to be considered.
Teo was run over by a car permanently damaging his back legs.
As a double amputee, the dilemma creates a complicated web.
The owners describe how Teo makes their lives better.
Being energetic, stimulating and inspiring, he provides them a lot of pleasure.
He is the best version of himself, something we all should strive to be.
The Wizard decides to create two devices to help Teo become free.
Teo and the Wizard teach us that with faith, courage and trust
Along with determination, we will find a way to readjust.
He develops a cart for Teo's back legs to run on hard surfaces.
But another invention is needed for Teo to complete his metamorphosis.
So a Frisbee-type system is made for the beach and water.
A miracle takes place because the Wizard did not falter
To give Teo a chance to run and play with this first-of-a-kind device.
Because the Wizard believes that every animal deserves a good life.
This story will strike a chord in your heart
A joy that only a small dog like Teo can impart.

Magical Creatures and Silver Linings

An Animal Sanctuary in Hawaii is providing hope for the world
By rescuing animals in need and providing a life that's deserved.
When we give animals a chance and families unite together good things happen
Miracles occur by treating all God's creatures with love and compassion.
A better life for all is put in place
Sometimes a little push is needed to finish the race.
We can continue to try no matter how long that it takes
Not being afraid to fail at first and make a few mistakes.
We learn from animals because they are strong
They fight through rough times and keep moving on.
When disabled or paralyzed they are incredibly resilient
They trust completely and remain amazingly persistent.

The Wizard introduces several of these magical creatures to you.
There's a Great Dane, paralyzed from meningitis, named Hank
A lamb, named Menina, walks again with the Wizard's help to thank.
Gaia is a sheep, rescued with her baby, Felicia, after severe neglect
She lost her leg and developed curvature of the spine as an effect.
The Wizard worked diligently to achieve something great
With the specialized braces and prosthetics he was able to create
To give these animals a chance to regain mobility and live a good life.
We are mesmerized by how he changes dire situations from dark to light.
The Wizard's nurturing nature for these magical creatures is unmatched
Working along side the family these transformations are dispatched.
The Wizard is dedicated to showing that silver linings are achievable
By conceiving the inconceivable and believing in the unbelievable.

The Unifying Factor

Colby is a rescue dog who becomes the unifying factor
For a blended family that is the lucky benefactor.
Colby was born with a congenital deformity.
Helping Colby to have a normal life is a top priority.
The bones in his front paw are not in the right place.
Colby's dire situation becomes the Wizard's new challenging case.
Animals of this nature are usually discarded
So when the Wizard arrives to help Colby he immediately gets started.
As time goes on muscle atrophy will set in affecting Colby's mobility.
Not able to support his body on just three legs decreases Colby's agility.
The Wizard answers the call to change Colby's quality of life.
He first gets to know the family members and seeks their advice
To understand Colby's role in the family and how he helps them to grow
Developing resiliency through the love and support they show.
The Wizard creates a unique and intricate prosthetic for his paw
To encapsulate and accommodate the crazy angles he saw.
Another miracle occurs for an animal and family in need
Acceptance of the foreign new leg is required to succeed.
Colby has to learn how to navigate on four legs instead of three
So that he finally can live a more normal life and run free.

Bringing Loving Hearts Together

What can you learn from animals with special needs
Is it their strong fighting spirit that helps them to proceed?
Boots and Buttercup have an abundance of enthusiasm and patience
Even though these two corgis face many physical limitations.
A caring and dedicated family decided to call
On the Wizard to try to improve the corgis' mobility
And provide a chance for them to live a life with more versatility.
That's what the Wizard does; he facilitates new chances
For a healthier life for animals using his creative medical advances.
Rex and Penny are two more dogs the Wizard assisted.
The kindness and genuine love for animals he shows is infectious.
He Improves lives with his carefully made prostheses and carts
Along with the gentleness and professionalism he imparts.
The Wizard travels next to a farm for rescued animals.
Here he meets an alpaca with very difficult parameters.
By creating special braces, she is able to move forward more normally.
The Wizard is able to straighten and stabilize her legs to achieve conformity.
This is what the Wizard continues to do.
His gift of listening is magical and it is definitely true
That he understands the needs of every animal he encounters.
The Wizard brings loving hearts together by his God-given powers
Bestowing hope and promise to families and animals in need
With confidence and belief that he can and will succeed.

The Underdogs

Can a cow and a dog both be an underdog?
You decide if this dog and a cow deserve such applause.
But don't expect them to win first place in a race or contest
Because these two animals are definitely not like all the rest.
They each have special needs as you will plainly see
And oddly enough they both share the name Penelope.
Penelope is a dog with scoliosis—
A severe curvature of the spine that's hard not to miss.
Her back legs have debilitating nerve damage
Making it unlikely to survive with this disadvantage.
Penelope the cow has a different mobility situation—
Part of her hoof was amputated causing an acute infection.
The owner and her neighbor are trying to do all they can.
Luckily they call on the Wizard to lend a helping hand
Knowing he believes they deserve more than just a glance.
The Wizard is challenged to find a way to give them a second chance.
First, for the dog he constructs a 3-wheel cart that's one of a kind
Then makes a boot sturdy enough to support the cow so not left behind.
While watching this transformation you realize that with God's grace
Something special is happening as you witness miracles taking place.
You'll find yourself rooting for these underdogs in this "amazing race."
They overcome the battle of their lives and are given a new start
With the expertise of the Wizard and all who offered their heart.

Buddies for Life

Pets and little kids have a unique awareness;
They treat each person with equal fairness.
Tenderness and kindness carries them a long way;
Feeling loved throughout each night and every day.
When necessary, they exhibit a strong fighter spirit;
Like underdogs who beat the odds and don't want the credit.
They become a family's unifying factor in so many ways,
By enjoying the simple things in life without having a say.
Happiness surrounds them when given enough attention;
Their enthusiasm is contagious adding a bright new dimension.
They strike a chord with your heart strings whenever they are near;
Unconditional love is a two-way street as it eventually does appear.
Animals can join loving hearts together with their presence;
As a part of the family, winsomeness constitutes their essence.
They give the home a spark of energy and increased liveliness,
As close bonds are forming, there is a feeling of peacefulness.
Pets are always ready to adapt to any situation they face,
By giving and receiving an affectionate and protective embrace.
Eventually you and your pet become buddies for life;
Just like a new baby, they produce a feeling of unplanned delight.

Finding Your Capabilities

To lift up and heal and put a smile on your face
Is exactly what the Wizard aims to embrace.
He will soon take a trip to Thailand
To an elephant nature park where he lends a hand.
It is one of the biggest undertakings of his career
Don't worry no spoiler alerts are you going to hear.

Wesley is a dog who has a severe deformity to one of his front legs
Okay for now but could later become a potential powder keg.
His family lives for the outdoors and loves to go skiing and hiking.
Wesley is a part of the family so he goes along even when water rafting.
After a little dogie yoga he turns into an adrenaline junkie.

The story of Wesley showcases his ability rather than his disability.
Wesley needs a special prosthesis with elbow suspension for extra mobility.
It's a challenge to maintain suspension while keeping uniformity.
With the Wizard's skill and expertise the special prosthesis is designed.
It can't be too heavy so he develops a fix that maintains a line
Between comfort, mobility and suspension that is one of a kind.
From this story we learn that to find your capabilities
It takes courage, determination and faith.
Wesley's family demonstrated all of these
Along with a special kinship not easy to explain.

Boone the Raccoon

The Wizard has treated and helped over 35,000 animals to have a better life
By nurturing hope and making the animal world auroral and bright.
In his next story, the Wizard meets Boone the Raccoon
At a Sanctuary in Kentucky where his objective comes in tune.
Injured animals and those with deformities get a new chance here.
The owners have a heartfelt mission that to them is very clear.
They teach that the coexistence of all life takes place in the environment.
Their goal is to heal and release injured animals to spread enlightenment.
They believe every animal has a place or purpose in the ecosystem
Forming a major part of the sanctuary's belief in this wisdom.
Boone's physical impairment prevents him from being released and to stay alive.
He has cerebellar hypoplasia and is unable to move normally and survive.
This is the first time the Wizard has made a cast for a raccoon, a wild animal.
Boone's current cart steers in a circle to the left so movement is unnatural
And Boone has a hard time getting the wheels to go over sticks and rocky terrain.
The Wizard faces a challenge requiring a lot of knowledge he has yet to gain.
He has to adjust the wheels to get the right angle creating a definitive design.
Different angles and alterations are taken into account for the cart to align.
The final cart has head lights and a redesign that solves the steering problem
And it also frees Boone's front legs for his new mobility to blossom.
From the story of Boone we learn that life is full of purpose
By taking a leap of faith your purpose will begin to surface.
When you find your purpose life expands in ways unimaginable.
Boone helps children to believe in dreams once inconceivable.
Surprisingly, many lives are touched by Boone's story.
And once again the tenacity of the Wizard ends in miraculous glory.

Watson and Peaches

This story features Watson, a dog, and Peaches, a goat.
The Wizard helps animals in need by uplifting and keeping them afloat.
Watson was hit by a car and needs a full-limb prosthetic design.
It has the lowest success rate because it is difficult to adjust to this kind.
A full-leg prosthesis is the most foreign to an animal and hardest to make.
The Wizard will go slow at the fitting because there is so much at stake.
He doesn't want Watson to freak out and not be able to adjust and accept.
It will be difficult for him to put his leg down and take the first step.
But something amazing happens; he gradually starts walking.
Of all the full-length prostheses the Wizard has made, only two animals have taken off right away without balking.

Peaches, the goat, lives at an animal rescue refuge in Connecticut.
He is not a house pet but a "pet that fits in the house" and not always so delicate.
Just because he's a goat doesn't mean he deserves less so it may seem intangible.
But he's more than just a goat to them; he's a friend so it's understandable.
Peaches has no range of motion because of a congenital deformity
Affecting his ligaments and hind legs so designing a cart is a priority.
It is a very tough build for the Wizard and a huge challenge.
It has to be light weight so Peaches can regain strength and balance.
Peaches definitely deserves a life worth living
Therefore no victory is too small to celebrate achieving.
Peaches shows how the most difficult challenges reap the greatest rewards.
With perseverance, Peaches gets fitted with a cart and hope is restored.
When you work hard, put forth the effort, and faith is inherent,
The greatness of people, the strength and courage of animals
And the brilliance and dedication of a craftsman become very apparent.

Are You a Dog or Cat Person?

Are you a dog person or a cat person?
Maybe you're really not certain.
In another Wizard story you meet Angus and Lux,
A cat and a dog who had to learn how to trust.
Lux, the dog, lost his leg due to abuse.
For this sweet little dog, there is no excuse.
Angus, the cat, has had multiple amputations.
We have to ask why this happens to one of God's creations.
Lux and Angus both want to be loved like all the others
And they are, by a loving family with two dedicated young brothers.
The owners are people who rescue pets in need.
It is their mission to adopt these animals and help them succeed.
Lux was found tied to a pole in cold weather, his fur all matted;
Circulation cut off to his front leg, which had to be amputated.

As he walks laboriously like a much older dog, we understand why
The family deeply feels they owe it to Lux to at least try.
It is very traumatic because many animals never get back on track
With love and tender care Lux and Angus are able to come back.
Angus, the cat, has a story that is one for the books
He has only one weight-bearing leg in the front when you take a look.
Both his front paws were so damaged
That it is a wonder how he has managed.
Rough things happened to Angus but he still has a capacity to survive
It was a hard life for a cat but because of a strong will he stays alive.
The entire family believes every living thing deserves a chance.
Seeing the complex problems that animals face,
They remain compelled to take a stance.
The Wizard tries to create a prosthetic for Angus' weight-bearing leg that is lightweight
So he doesn't reject it because of his sensitive state.
At first he walks gingerly then suddenly takes off much to our surprise
As a cat's life is transformed right before our eyes.
A custom fit, full-leg prosthesis for Lux is difficult for the Wizard to make.
It will be a challenge for Lux and a risk that the Wizard is willing to take.
To ensure Lux can push through the anxiety and build confidence
Adjusting to these new legs and paws will require divine providence.
In this story we witness how lives are transformed when there is hope.
Once again, the Wizard performs two miracles of a magnificent scope.
Now can you better answer the original question—
Are you a dog person, a cat person or maybe just a new fan?
The Wizard seems lost for words
So he just shouts out "SHAZAM!"
And that says it all, bam!

The Other Side of the Fence

We all want to be part of something and belong
Not be stuck on the "other side of the fence" for too long.
To lift up and heal is what the Wizard aims to achieve
Miracles happen when desire mixes with determination and we believe.
This story is about Timmy and Poppy who are sure to impress you
An odd pair who live on a ranch in California for rescues.
Timmy is a sheep and Poppy a goat who must stay on the other side of the fence
Because both have special rehabilitation needs that are difficult and intense.
Timmy is seven months old with infected joints and has to walk on his knees
Because an infection caused his two front knees to lock up and freeze.
Poppy's front leg collapses at the wrist of his knee not allowing him to flex.
To be able to walk on all fours is the goal that determines what to do next.
The Wizard creates special designs for Poppy and Timmy to give them a new chance.
It's unbelievable to experience this transformation that at first glance
Seems too good to be true but we are witnessing a true phenomenon
As they start to walk on their new legs cementing their common bond.
The Wizard's corrective builds do more than give animals mobility
He changes lives creating a bright new-world acceptability
Which enables Timmy and Poppy to join the rest for some animal fun.
Being on the "other side of the fence" is a dream and a miracle rolled into one.

Marvelous Millie and Shoofly Pie

Marvelous Millie lives in Pennsylvania at a family farm.
Millie is a 3-year-old golden retriever who becomes a good luck charm.
Even though born with a front leg deformity, she is excited about life.
She has helped her owners through tough times and strife.
Millie's owner was involved in a serious motorcycle accident several years ago.
She now has a prosthetic leg, the same side as Millie's so it goes to show
Life throws curveballs, things happen beyond our control that we must face.
But then the events that took place for the owner were purely a sign of grace.
The owner's speed of recovery and how she managed expectations were crucial.
Without Millie to relate to, her situation could have been more futile.
God had a plan for Millie and her owner; they were put together for a reason
Due to similar situations with their legs they developed a sense of cohesion.
Everyone fighting together persistently became the driving factor.
Entitled to take a break, the Wizard tried some shoofly pie as a simple distractor.
Afterward he got back to work and made Millie's mold and cast.
He had to align and put an extension in the right spot for it to last.
It is more than just a leg; both Millie and her owner were awarded a second chance.
When inspiration and hope come together, we use what we have experienced and
learned in order to move forward and advance.

Eeny, Meeny, Miny, Moe

Eeny, meeny, miny, moe,
Catch a camel by the toe.
If he hollers, let him go,
Eeny, meeny, miny, moe.

This counting-out children's rhyme has us asking the question—
What does Bentley, Kala, Moe, and Roo have in common?

Bentley is a rescue dog adopted from a kill shelter
The Wizard is helping him to live a life that will be stellar.
Bentley requires braces to provide greater mobility.
The Wizard helps him to have legs that will allow him more agility.
When Bentley takes off it is a feeling the Wizard will never forget
Because Bentley's owners now have a happier, healthier pet.

Kala is a small puppy who was badly wounded
Found on the streets of India but not excluded
By a family in Florida who rescued and gave her special care.
She was born with forelimb deformities and was in great despair.
Her new family wants to help her walk again and find a forever home
She can't run fast, suffers from anxiety, but now will never be left alone.
The Wizard needs to develop two different braces, which is an extra challenge.
He does wonders in helping pets like Kala rebalance
And regain confidence so their lives are fulfilled.
The Wizard's prosthetics and braces demonstrate his transformational skills.

Moe is a dromedary happy-go-lucky camel who is very bold.
He is a sweetheart who was bottle fed at seven weeks old.
His feet are floppy because of dropped ankle tendons that shifted forward.
His front legs collapse so when he moves it is very awkward.
The goal for Moe is to be able to stand and support his massive weight.
The Wizard has never cast a camel before so being here to try must be fate.
He is like a shining light of hope for Moe as he searches for a solution.
Since Moe's legs are folded under, reinforced steel toe straps are used as a resolution.
It was a tough road to recovery, but Moe mastered his prosthetics quickly.
With the will to live, strength, and motivation a camel miracle occurs atypically
Reminding us that physical limitations shouldn't hold us back from a fulfilling life.
Happy to be rolling in grass again Moe enjoys this new-found delight.

Roo is a one-year-old chihuahua born with only two back legs
This adorable little ball of energy makes us pause to appreciate these threads—
The threads of life called blessings that we take for granted
Often failing to give thanks for the gifts we have been handed.
Patience is required for the Wizard to create and adjust wheels for Roo.
God is always listening as we see Roo take off on wheels that are new.
Before the Wizard can build any device he needs to build trust
Always putting the needs of his patients first helping them to adjust.
That's definitely the case in the stories of these animals
So what do Bentley, Kala, Moe, and Roo have in common that is tangible?
They all star in amazing stories of triumph often seeming too good to be true
Then we realize it is the Wizard's dedication and skills that stand out as the glue.

Gentle Giants

From experiences in life, we learn to stand strong
Never giving up if we want to begin to right what is wrong.
Elephants are gentle giants who never forget
They are like us in spirit and can be easily upset.
When mistreated their dignity is swept aside
Emotional stress and anxiety are not easy to hide.
Trust must be established so healing can begin
Then the recovery process can start from within.
Like humans it is hard for elephants to forget the past
Helping them to overcome torture and abuse is possible at last.

The Wizard travels to Thailand on a mission
Working to alleviate physical and mental disabilities on his epic expedition.
In Thailand he meets elephants Mae Mai, Khun Dej and a bull named Mr. Cow.
Mr. Cow was born with 2 front legs missing so the Wizard has to begin now
To find a way to help him regain and maintain his balance and strength.
He works tirelessly to learn, understand and study the culture in depth.
While building prosthetics for these animals, the Wizard faces several challenges.
Many of the elephants have severe limb, spinal deformities and imbalances.
For Mae Mai, the Wizard designs a stylish new leg brace
And at this elephant nature park he witnesses several miracles take place.
For example, he watches as Mae Mai takes her first steps
Experiencing the joy of being an elephant again as life becomes less complex.
He realizes it was a struggle and a long road to recovery
But when she walks to the mud bath he witnesses her victory lap of discovery.
The Wizard discovers why this is a very good day
Because a better life is attainable for many animals especially for Khun Dej.
The perseverance of these elephants is an inspiration to us all
Elephants love each other unconditionally and always answer the call
They look after and take care of each other until they die.
We should learn from them and not have to ask why
We can't love each other regardless of our differences.
These gentle giants demonstrate that the walls we build lack significance.

All For the Love of Bubba

When God puts animals in our path we have a responsibility
To take care of them the best we can within our capability.
That's how it was for Bubba, a special dog with special needs
Whose owners do everything possible to help him succeed.
Bubba is a unique pet who was lucky to find a loving home
Where he is treated like a son and will never be left alone.
He walks on three legs, which requires extra care
And his owners have an abundance to spare
For this bully mix who always has a "dog" smile on his face
And a zest and love for life that can't be erased.
Bubba is called the karate dog, an unusual name
When looking at him tears may come down like rain.
The Wizard travels far to help Bubba live a life without struggle and pain
So when a martial arts master meets the prosthetics master there is a lot to gain.
After a short visit to Santa Monica the Wizard arrives
Ready to make a wrist brace and a full prosthesis that the situation requires.
Casting his full leg for a prosthesis will be very difficult.

Bubba is a vulnerable creature, which is significant
Because he is short, stout and low to the ground
He puts too much pressure on his body as he runs around
Causing wear and tear on the wrist of his arthritic leg
So the health of his legs has been like a powder keg.
Anticipation mounts while the Wizard works
It takes time and precision to work out the quirks.
Both the Wizard and Bubba need the perfect design
So when Bubba leans into the prosthesis it is a positive sign.
Trying out the silicone-lined wrist brace is next
Bubba is strong and determined but how he reacts is complex.
We see how energy and enthusiasm create sheer magnificence
When there is unconditional love making all the difference.
Life should be lived to the fullest regardless of handicaps and problems.
Bubba has been given a lifeline to grasp onto so a new leash on life blossoms.

Be Brave Amelia

In this story, a cow named Amelia lives at an animal sanctuary and farm—
A special place that promotes awareness of the mistreatment of animals
protecting them from harm.
Animals on this farm are given an abundance of kindness and love
They are never forgotten when there is hope and help from above.
It provides forever homes for abused, neglected, unwanted and/or homeless
barnyard animals.
The Wizard travels to Washington state bringing his expertise and other
intangibles.
He is asked to build a brace for Amelia who was born with leg deformities.
Designing a prosthetic to help lengthen her life is one of his main priorities.
Due to an infection, Amelia's legs are crooked and she is blind.
Amelia is considered to be the face of the farm and is one of a kind.
The shelter adopted Amelia when she was ten days old
She had to be bottle fed as her story is told.
Amelia will not have a future if walking continues to cause pain

And as her weight increases, her legs will be under too much strain.
She will be two-and-a-half years old soon so it is perfect timing
Perhaps a divine intervention with the stars all aligning
For the Wizard to work miracles and give Amelia his best shot
At having a life where she can play in the pasture and be able to trot.
Her four legs weren't cooperating to make that possible
With three crooked legs and a shorter back leg it was improbable.
Casting a cow like Amelia will be challenging for sure
It can be dangerous unless there is trust and she feels secure.
The Wizard works tirelessly to make one brace with a lift
His incredible talents used in this difficult endeavor is truly a gift.
The Wizard never gives up to ensure that Amelia's story has a happy ending
A break that otherwise would always be pending.
Together the Wizard and Amelia have many challenges to overcome
So be brave Amelia, with the Wizard's help the best is yet to come.

Compassionate Habits and Actions

Having faith and patience opens the door for something better
So that animals and people can live in harmony together.
Wise actions of the Wizard have become compassionate habits
That give animals and their owners hope and balance.

Valentine is a pot belly pig with a front limb deformity.
Because of someone's love for animals and nonconformity
She was rescued from neglect by a compassionate caregiver
Who caters to all of Valentine's needs and cherishes her.
Valentine's story is just one of the lessons learned from the Wizard
Here are a few more insights that should be considered.

Pigs like people will squeal
To tell you how they feel.

Stay positive, don't sit around feeling sorry for yourself
In all circumstances, realize the gift of good health.

Animals have different personalities
In all different situations and localities.

Many people treat animals like family
They share their lives and do so happily.

You can let dire situations eat you alive or reach for a solution
There is always a higher power involved with the resolution.

Champion is a quadriplegic cow
You may wonder why and how.

Look with your heart not your eyes
Touch, love, and help are words that are wise
So when healing occurs it is not a surprise.

Discovering what makes you different makes you special.
Special-needs animals have so much untouched potential.
They are more than just their disabilities
Providing many challenging possibilities.
Every living thing including animals are worthy
With the Wizard's help, they can start a new journey.

Animals have more depth than your eyes can see
Each one has a super power that was meant to be.
You can find an animal's specialness
As you discover there is strength in sameness.
Animals with disabilities are magical
Helping them to live a better life is never fanatical
It demonstrates a true labor of love
That uses help from a source from above.

Chip is a sheep and Winnie is a dog with similar problems
Because they have bonded it speaks volumes.
Anyone can see that they love each other like a sister and brother
They share like disabilities and are sensitive to each other.
The Wizard will help them fulfill their potential
Knowing his actions are enormously consequential.
He begins by focusing on their leg muscles and spines
So he is able to create new and innovative designs.
Chip and Winnie's story shows that no matter what you go through
There are always others with tough situations too
Therefore, it is natural and organic to form a bond.
Life is all about balance and how you respond.

What you give out will come back to you
Knowing this helps to pull you through.
If you have compassion in your heart
Karma is believed to play a part.
Then being a voice for an animal becomes second nature
Your positive energy will return to you like a favor.
When you are doing something good in life
Kindness leads to trust that eases the strife.

We all want to be loved, respected, and acknowledged
Compassionate habits grow and expand our knowledge.
If you look for it, there is virtue and goodness in the world
And when animals are seen as worthy, then hope is unfurled.

Diego and Birdie

Diego is a Flemish Giant rabbit—
The largest breed of rabbit in the world.
Diego was injured as a baby when his problem unfurled.
His leg was broken above the elbow and didn't heal
So he wasn't able to live with a bunny's normal zeal.
The Wizard traveled to Illinois to help and serve
By designing a light prosthesis for Diego that is curved.
Now he is a bunny with a prosthesis, the only one in the world
Diego doesn't react negatively when he takes it for a whirl.
Birdie is a wire-haired dog who has never walked on all fours.
The Wizard visits this close-knit family to learn the allure
Of Birdie's influence and prominence as the unifying factor—
A testament to gratitude and appreciation of a true adaptor.
The Wizard makes a full-length prosthesis with padding at the bone
Birdie loves being outside, this is when she is in her zone.
There is a fear that her good front leg may break down at the shoulder
As time goes on and she gets older.
From Birdie's story we learn that we all need to be lifted up
Life is more than one person that needs help like this pup.
Their strong faith gets them through hard times
They are a generous family, seemingly one of a kind.
Fostering babies is one way they choose to give back
Birdie and their three daughters help them to keep on track
Showing that the world doesn't revolve just around you
Birdie binds them together and becomes the family's glue.

Thirteen is a Lucky Number

When it concerns 13 incredible animals, 13 is a lucky number.
As they search for answers to dire situations it will not encumber
The Wizard who believes nothing is impossible when you believe you can
Even when he faces a difficult challenge to solve in a short time span.

When you meet these animals who all have special needs
You will forget about all the world's unfettered greed.
Thirteen owners came to L.A. hoping for an answer to complications
For their pet's mobility problems and unique situations.

The Wizard started meeting each one to establish their needs
Then talk to the owners and follow their lead
Adding to his goal of helping animals to walk again
The Los Angeles pop-up workshop had now begun.

One of the lucky 13, Maggie, is a 1-year old dog
Who suffers from a severe problem of mobility
The Wizard quickly analyzed her situation
And made a diagnosis to the best of his ability.

Rocket is another one of the animals rescued
He couldn't balance at all when first viewed.
It was determined that Rocket has swimmer syndrome
Where his legs fanned out as he has grown.
Currently his chest touches the ground.
A customized cart is the best solution that the Wizard found.

Also there is Bey (short for Beyoncé) who also needs help.
Bey is 8 weeks old and she's a diva of sorts
She has cerebellar hypoplasia,

Sprawling front legs that don't support.
She would bounce backwards with a cart
Because she has no side-to-side control.
To prolong the life of all these animals
And keep them healthy is the Wizard's goal.

Frida is a 2-year-old dog who had a very dark trauma
Resulting in weak back legs causing quite a drama
As she walks only on her back legs to allow space for resilience.
Frida deserves to be able to walk again and have that experience.

Chetak is a dog who fractured his spine leaving him paralyzed
He needs a cart that will suspend his legs
So its design needs to be very specialized.

Cashew is another dog with chronic pain in 3 legs
He needs prosthetics to extend his joints to help them mend
And a cart and braces to complete his incredible transformation.
Achieving this improbable mission is truly an inspiration.

This mission requires faith in believing that there is hope
Because most of these animals were found at the end of their rope.
They had to constantly adapt and change their perspective.
The Wizard's experience lends well to this incredible objective.

Using ingenuity the Wizard diligently works to make all the molds in 3 days
His keen sense of determining need is worthy of praise.
The workshop and its results will help to build awareness
Proving that animals with limitations can live and be treated with fairness.
This becomes evident as these animals give back more than they give
So at the Fundraiser, they walked proudly down the "red carpet"
Excited to be free and to live.

Acknowledgments

Debbie Campana

My awesome and dedicated editor and friend who has read, critiqued and edited every poem in this book. Without her none of these poems wold have come to fruition.

Phyllis Schechtman

My proof reader and friend who reads and approves all of my poems. She is my cheerleader and lends a hand whenever needed.

My Family

Special thanks to my husband Michael Yankus who passed away on January 9th, 2024 and miss every single day. Thanks also to my family that includes my children and grandchildren, which includes Jennifer Caldwell, Stephen Caldwell, Andrew Caldwell and their spouses, Peter Farah, Liberty Caldwell and Stephanie Caldwell, and eight grandchildren: Nyah, Layla, Kira, John, Finley, Evelyn, Hudson and Quinn.

My Forever Friends and Pep 'R Uppers

Debbie, Phyllis, Bonnie, Pat, Valerie, Carol, Jean and Judy also known as the Dancing Divas who inspire me to keep writing.

All My Line Dance Friends and Teachers

My Mentors

Wanda, Rachel and Kelly from The Pregnancy and Family Care Center

My College Friends

Barbara, Sheila and Joanne who encourage me to keep writing

About the Author

Barbara C. Welsh is a poet, editor, and retired teacher among many other accomplishments.

She started writing poetry during the COVID-19 pandemic. She was learning a new dance on line when she wrote her first poem called *"Hoping, Praying, and Dancing."* Since then she has written over 420 poems, many of which have been published in The Villages Daily Sun, Poet's Corner and the Village Neighbors Magazine. Her first book, *"One Bright Day"* was published in 2022 and her second book, *"Sell Yourself a Smile"* published in 2023, are both sold on Amazon.com, Barnes & Noble.com, and Walmart.com.

Barbara loves to dance especially line dancing, Zumba, and more recently cardio drumming. She was in the Gemstone Dancers, a performing dance group, and is a volunteer counselor at the Pregnancy and Family Care Center in Leesburg, Florida.

A member of The Florida Authors & Publishers Association (FAPA), Florida Writers Association (FWA), the Writers League of The Villages (WLOV), and Associate Member of the Academy of American Poets, Barbara has a Bachelor of Science degree in Home Economics and Education from West Virginia Wesleyan College and a Master of Arts degree in Family Studies from Montclair State University in N.J.

Barbara lives in The Villages, Florida. She has three children, four stepchildren and eighteen grandchildren.

Contact her at Barbaratwoten@gmail.com

Or on her website at dancesoflifepoetry.com

About the Illustrator

Amber has loved drawing and art her entire life. She worked her way through college as a Dell computer technician and in 2003 earned an AA in Art and an AS in Graphic Design from Santa Fe and Lake City Community Colleges, respectively. She went on to learn the ins and outs of graphic design, pre-press, and print production in the field for 15 years.

Since starting ALL Illustration & Design in 2018, she has helped many independent authors illustrate, design, and self-publish their stories, and she would love to help you! Amber lives in North Central Florida with her daughter, her cats, and a serious art supply collection.

Check out her portfolio at www.amberleighluecke.com

www.ingramcontent.com/pod-product-compliance
Lightning Source LLC
Chambersburg PA
CBHW021626120626
46545CB00002B/410